Workplace Investiga

CW01508576

A Novel Approach

B. Max Dubroff
SPHR, SHRM-SCP

Christine Cave
Esq., SPHR, SHRM-SCP

Cover and chapter illustrations by Sarah Dubroff

DISCLAIMERS:

This book is intended to provide readers with practical, helpful information about conducting workplace investigations. Although the authors have made every effort to ensure that the information in this book was correct and current as of the time of publication, they disclaim any liability for any losses or disruption caused by errors or omissions, regardless of whether such errors or omissions resulted from negligence or any other cause.

Nothing contained in the book should be considered legal advice and no attorney-client relationship is formed between you and the authors. The laws discussed in the book are subject to, and indeed frequently undergo, revision that may significantly change an employer's obligations or employees' rights. The book is not a substitute for legal advice and you are encouraged to consult appropriate legal counsel regarding your specific situation.

All names and events in the story are fictitious. Any resemblance to actual persons or events is coincidental.

Table of Contents

Preface

Is this a worthwhile book for *you* to read?

If you work with imperfect people—particularly if you are a Human Resources (HR) professional—the answer is a resounding, "Yes!"

One thing we know about imperfect people is those imperfections come to life, often in ways that do not fit our organization's values or policies. This can result in small conflicts or breaches that need an inquiry, or larger and more complex situations that require a significant commitment of resources to determine the facts. At both ends of the spectrum and every point between, the process by which you gather information and resolve disputed facts, is an investigation.

Whether you might occasionally do an investigation, do investigations frequently, or provide counsel or manage people who do investigations, this book is useful for you! It provides information and a perspective that can help you get started with your first investigation or improve upon your existing knowledge and experience if you have conducted investigations before.

While reading this book is not enough for you to become an expert investigator, it can be a significant element in your personal and professional development. Along with improving your understanding of investigations and the development of investigation processes, it can increase your confidence to do the right thing.

This book provides practical examples and illustrations consistent with a risk management approach that goes beyond typical risk-aversion to understanding and managing risk. It also emphasizes critical thinking and systems thinking as core principles. These principles drive the focus through the immediate impacts and prompt you to consider the secondary and tertiary impacts of your actions.

Our investigation process model goes beyond a basic checklist for conducting investigations by providing an integrated process. This process is better suited to handle the real-life situations that require prioritizing, scheduling, and judgment than a simple checklist, particularly on the most challenging days.

Our model has four main phases. The following phase doesn't start until the previous one is completed; but, once a phase starts, it continues through the process. For example, while a good investigator would not conduct interviews prior to developing questions, a great investigator will develop additional questions while interviews are progressing.

Assessing	Planning	Understanding	Completing
Decide to investigate	Be quick, thorough and objective	Stay focused	Document the investigation
Address safety	Select the investigator	Gather & evaluate evidence	Reach a conclusion
Maintain confidentiality	Plan the investigation	Conduct interviews	Take action
	Prepare questions	Determine credibility	Follow up

The duration of the phases will vary with the complexity of the investigations. For example, the "Understanding" phase will be much shorter when the evidence and responsibility are clear versus when there is little evidence and key facts conflict.

There are times the order of the steps could be modified, but you should carefully consider the impact before making any changes to the process. For example, you will accept evidence provided at any time, including when receiving the complaint. However, actively looking for and evaluating evidence prior to developing a sound investigative plan will result in a less efficient and effective investigation.

This book has four main chapters, aligned with the four phases of the process model. Each chapter begins with a story illustrating several investigations in an organization, and is followed by a discussion of each step in the phase, with details, recommendations, and concerns to consider.

Let's meet our protagonist and her team ...

Chapter 1
Michelle's Monday Morning Mayhem

"Maybe Marie's Monday morning meeting marathon madness might morph moderately?" I muse as the company staff meeting hits its stride into the third straight hour. I do what I can to stay engaged in the meetings, and an occasional alliteration with my favorite letter brings quiet joy. After all, because my initials are "MMM," it's going to occasionally enter my mind, right?

I appreciate being part of the most important discussions and decisions in the company, but if they could just plan an occasional break ... the numbness in my legs after sitting so long cannot be ignored. And I admit that my attention starts to drift a little, particularly each time my cell phone has vibrated, covertly alerting me to a call or message.

Because my role as the HR Director means numerous calls for assistance from the company's site managers, I know the first thing I'll do when the meeting adjourns is check to see what's going on. And—like magic, good timing, or good luck— just then, Marie suggests a break. Let's see that phone ... oh, wow! Six calls from Chris, my Assistant HR Director. I'll call her first. She picks up before the first ring is complete; she was waiting on me.

"Michelle! Did you get my voicemail?" Chris asks right away. "Probably not; I know you were busy," Chris continues, "so, the big deal is that I'm at the North site and Wendy accused

Roger of sexual harassment right before I could counsel her on her lateness."

"Roger!? Oh, man," I say. Roger, the janitor, is a good worker, but was the subject of a previous complaint for arguing with a department manager and the site manager. "I really hoped the reprimand would have worked and he wouldn't break any other rules ... Wait! I take that back; let's get the details first," knowing just because it was reported doesn't make it fact and the two incidents may not be related.

"Right!" Chris says, "Actually, *my* immediate thought was that Wendy knew she was in trouble for something and that she picked on someone who couldn't defend himself because of his limited mental capacity. But, I knew I was ahead of myself, so I just wrote that thought in my notes, to follow-up on later. I don't want that thought to distract me from the investigation, but didn't want to forget to follow up on it, either, you know what I mean? Anyway, Wendy just started her written statement and I'll make sure it is as detailed as the verbal complaint she told the manager and me. She gave an exact date, a 15-minute time window, and said she went straight to Pat and told her about it right after it happened ... and she gave a detailed location of the incident—at the doorway of the break room, which should be right in the view of a camera. I've yet to discuss confidentiality or whether she feels a safety risk."

"Chris, you're on it!" I say with a big smile. It's so great to have her on the team. "So, what were you calling for?"

"Just to make sure you're aware, mostly because of the friendship between Marie and Wendy. Also, to ask if you want Tyler to come be part of the investigation, because he's new and is learning our ways. But, I already called him and he's on his way. That's what you want, right?"

"Definitely! Call me when you have a plan."

"You got it, Michelle. Talk to you in about an hour," then Chris hangs up.

Now, let's check the voicemail. I see the ones from Chris; I'll listen to those later, just in case there is something she forgot to tell me or there might be something on which I can give her feedback. Well, the only other voicemail is from John, the site manager at our South site.

John's message is short, "Call me." Well, I have to get back into the meeting, and I don't know how urgent it is from that short message, so I run down the hall to the office of our HR Specialist, Sarah.

As soon as I enter, Sarah excitedly says, "Great! I was just writing an email. Do you want me to just tell you or would you rather read the email?"

"I have to get back to the conference room. Just highlight anything urgent and we can discuss other details when I get out of my meeting," I say.

"Okay. Vernon from the East site called and said he thinks Billy is high or something," Sarah says.

I force a smile and say, "Okay, any reason why he thinks this?"

"Yup, Vernon said," Sarah makes finger quotes in the air, "'I have been around people who were high and this guy is high.' I knew that wasn't specific enough, so I asked him to describe the behaviors and how they were different than normal. Vernon said his eyes are bloodshot, his speech is sometimes slurred, he is saying weird things, and he is having a hard time standing straight or still."

Sarah had done well! Just last month, the group training was on the importance of getting details about the behaviors and not just labels, like "under the influence."

"Okay, I'll be right back. Meanwhile, please make sure Vernon has Billy in a safe place, call Lance and ask him to go to the East site, and please call John at South. He left me a short voicemail and I don't know what he needs." I turn and walk back down the hall to find Marie.

"Marie!" I catch her before she enters the conference room. "We have two investigations that need our attention, so I wanted to find out whether I need to be in the next part of the meeting or if I could focus on these concerns."

"Is it anything I need to know about?" Marie asks.

"There is a complaint of sexual harassment from Wendy at the North location that Chris is working on and there is an employee suspected to be under the influence at the East location. Lance is on that side of town today, so I am sending him over. Meanwhile, I need to find out what John needs at South." I am suddenly aware that I am a little breathless from running down the hall ... I hope I don't sound nervous or unconfident.

"Okay. That seems more pressing than the marketing plan we will be discussing, even though it would help for you to be aware of the plan. Come back in once you get the chaos controlled." Marie turns to the conference room, then turns back, "Keep me updated on the situations, please."

"Will do," I say and turn back down the hall to Sarah's office. As I enter, I say, "Sarah, what does John at the South site need?"

Sarah grabs her note pad from the desk while starting, "There is a dispute between two employees, including threats made by both. The two involved are Sam and David—both great employees. John said that he has them separated and things are calm right now, but he requests HR support for this. I'd really like to go support whomever you have investigate this, because I know a little about both of them and I haven't done a 'he-said/he-said' case yet."

With hardly a pause, I say, "That's a great idea, Sarah. I think you will be great support for Lance on this. I'll call him now."

Sarah almost bounces around her desk to grab her purse, keys, phone and notebook. I dial Lance's phone. He answers and I can hear the noise of the road as he is driving. "Hello?" Lance says, a little louder than needed, but that's how he talks on that earpiece ... at least he's following our safety policy.

"Lance, where are you right now and can you head to the South site for an investigation?"

Lance replies, "I am just approaching the East site, but I can turn around and head South. Who will take care of the issue at the East site? Tyler?"

I say, "No, he's working on another case at the North site. I will call Vernon and work on a plan with him. I am sending Sarah to support you and she is leaving now. She will call with the details."

Lance says, "Okay, I'll keep you updated."

Now, I need to call Vernon at the East site. I call his office, he answers and I ask, "Do you have a minute to talk?"

Vernon replies calmly, "Yes. I have Billy right here with me in my office and we're waiting on Lance."

"I had to send Lance to handle another incident at the South site. If you are comfortable with the process on the substance abuse suspicion form, you could have another manager as your witness and handle this directly. Are you okay with that?"

Vernon says, "Sure. The form is easy and I'll get the department manager to sit in as a witness."

I know Vernon is smart and he follows guidance very well, so I'll leave it to him. "Great. Just call me at each of the decision points, please."

Vernon agrees and hangs up.

I use this moment of calm to make sure my calendar is clear, because I need to be available to my team.

Only a few moments later, my phone rings; it's Vernon. "Michelle, as soon as we sat down with Billy, he said, 'I won't pass a drug test.' I asked 'why,' and he said 'because I'm high.' I asked if he would write that down, he refused and said, 'I'm going home.' I asked him to let us call a cab for him and he agreed, so he is sitting here, waiting on the cab."

I say, "Okay, thanks, Vernon. Please give him the information on the employee assistance program, emphasize that he can use the services for up to a month from now and ask Billy again for a statement, just in case he has changed his mind. Either way, we'll need statements from both you and the department manager. Also, give him the phone number to HR;

tell him to contact us by Thursday so we can assess his employment status and whether he is eligible for rehabilitation."

Vernon says hesitantly, "I thought we have a zero tolerance policy for drug use."

I reply, "As a general rule, yes. However, we need to complete the investigation. Even though he admitted being under the influence at work, we take a moment to consider both this incident and its implications, particularly any possible relationship with addiction, disability, prevention, or other possible concerns."

Vernon sounds a little more relaxed, saying, "Okay. I just wanted to make sure we didn't change our culture for this one case."

I reply, "The primary difference is what we are telling him at the end of this interview. Previously, we had told people that their employment was immediately terminated; now, we tell them to contact HR so we have the opportunity to make sure we've gone through the process and considered all angles. We realized this opportunity for improvement at an employment law seminar last month."

Vernon asks, "Will you be training the managers on this new approach, so it doesn't surprise them, too?"

I reply, "Yes, we have that on the agenda. There is no change to our policy, so I see the opportunity to improve our practice immediately."

Vernon says, "Well, I appreciate you, Michelle. Talk to you later." And we hang up the phone.

Chris calls me a few minutes later and says, "Wendy did a great job on the statement. She wrote down every detail that she had told me. I'll read the main part: 'Four days ago, on Thursday, between 1:45pm and 2:00pm, as I was heading to the door to leave the break room, Roger stood in the doorway blocking me. He stared at my chest and said he liked me. He then reached out with both hands and touched my breasts and said, "I like these too." I pushed him aside, told him to never touch me again and went through the door. I saw Pat right after and told her what happened and she said Roger did the same thing to her just two days prior.'"

"I also did a written Q&A with her on another sheet, so I have even more details. For example, when I asked how she was certain about the time it occurred, she wrote that it was at the end of her usual afternoon break. When I asked why she waited four days to report the incident, she answered, 'I don't like the site manager and was waiting to see someone from HR.' I asked if there were any other concerns in the department and she wrote, 'Everything else is great in the department. We all get along great. Roger just needs to be told to be more professional.' I then asked whether she had any concerns being around Roger and she responded, 'He won't do it again. I am okay being around Roger.' Finally, I asked if there was anything else and she wrote, 'No.' I told her we will get right on this to find out what's going on and to contact me or you if there are any concerns. I concluded the interview, gave Wendy our standard assurance of confidentiality, and she indicated she understood. After she left, I created an investigative folder and wrote notes describing the sequence of events."

"I then discussed the situation with the site manager. She said she had not heard of any concerns with Roger's behavior. We called in the department manager who supervises Wendy and Pat; he said he had not heard anything at all, either. I told the managers that I would do the investigation and would tell them if I needed anything. I also reminded them of what to say if anyone asks about the investigation: ask where the information came from and assure the person that the organization takes this matter seriously and we are investigating it."

"Great job, Chris. Even though Wendy indicated no concerns, we need to make this our top priority. Video is normally retained for 30 days and it has only been four, so we should be okay. But, check the system right away just in case. Do we need to separate Roger from Wendy and Pat?"

Chris says, "Roger has already completed his shift and is gone for the day. He is also off tomorrow, so they won't be working together. Even though Wendy said she feels comfortable working together, we may need to revisit this when Roger returns to work later this week."

As soon as I hang up from the call with Chris, Lance calls. Without so much as a greeting, Lance launches in, "As I was walking in, I saw that Sarah had already arrived and she had an employee talking to her very excitedly. As I got closer, I could hear that the employee, Walter, was complaining about being cyber-bullied via text message by an employee of one of our suppliers, named Keith. Sarah did a great job; all I had to do was listen. She led him to an available office and I followed. She asked Walter if he still had the text messages; he said no.

She asked what was on the text messages and Walter just said, 'he was bullying me cyber-ly.' Sarah asked if he could remember any of the words from the texts and he said he could not. Sarah asked when he received the texts, and he said he wasn't sure, but it might have been around one to three months ago. Sarah asked why he is reporting it now, instead of when it happened, and Walter replied that he didn't know it was against the rules until he saw the anti-harassment video during a recent training. Sarah gave him her card and encouraged him to call her if anything happens or if he remembers details about the previous incident(s). He seemed satisfied." Lance stops to take a breath, then continues, "I'll tell you what was really satisfying, though; both the great job that Sarah did and the fact that our anti-harassment video has at least increased awareness. This is wonderful."

I beam with excitement, "That is great. Thank you for calling. When can Sarah get me a short report? I want to call the HR Director at the supplier's company and notify him or her of the complaint, but with the caveat that there is nothing to investigate at this time."

Lance says, "She can get it to you by 5:00pm today. We'll get to work on the reason we came and call you and let you know our plan." Lance terminates the call as abruptly as it began. I smile to myself.

I glance at the clock and realize Marie's meeting would have finished by now. I decide quickly to go to the North site to check on Chris' investigative plan, because Wendy's complaint is such a serious one.

As I am leaving the office, Lance calls again, this time with the assessment of the investigation into the employee altercation. "John said David's complaint is that Sam said, 'I'll beat you like a drum.' David also reported that every person in the department is getting impatient with him. Sam reported, however, that David said, 'I'll pound your head.' When John asked Sam what Sam had said to David, Sam said, 'All I said was to stop beating your drum and get back to work because he kept boasting about how great a job he does.' Both said they can work with the other person and they have cooled off. I'll work on an investigation plan and call you to discuss it in about 15 minutes."

"Great. Thank you, Lance."

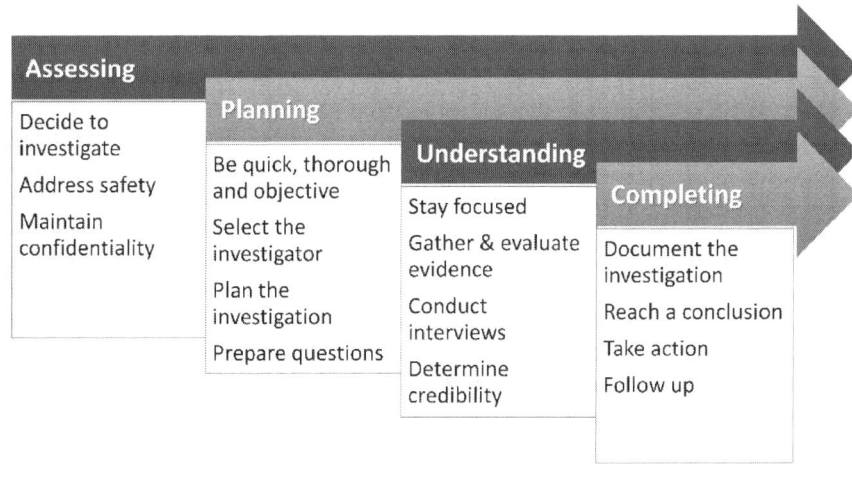

Assessing
Decide to investigate
Address safety
Maintain confidentiality

An investigation is a formal process by which you gather facts and resolve conflicts by making credibility determinations. It is not a substitute for coaching (although that may be a result), real-time feedback, or even taking corrective action when you directly observe inappropriate behavior. When presented with an issue, you will have to decide whether the issue warrants an investigation. You cannot do that until you obtain a full report of the complaint and determine if it is within your purview.

You should investigate when there is a report or suspicion of inappropriate or unlawful conduct or when someone has filed a legal or administrative action against your organization. An investigation should not be used simply to uncover a reason to fire someone. If you decide an investigation is warranted, you will need to decide the type of investigation needed, how quickly it must be undertaken, commit to seeing the investigation through, and establish an investigative file to get and stay organized. Let's look closer at the decision to investigate.

☐ **Get the report**

The initial report of concern can come from many different sources: a complainant who was affected by the alleged action, a witness aware of the alleged incident, a manager who has noticed something suspicious, a government agency that has received a report of wrongdoing, or any combination of these. The reporting person could be an employee (current, departing or former), customer, supplier, family or friend of the complainant, etc. You also may learn of the need to investigate from reviewing reports or other data, or the need for investigation may arise out of casual conversations with others—not a report or complaint per se, but from someone relaying a story that suggests possible unlawful activity or gross misconduct has occurred.

> 👁 Through the complaint by Wendy, Michelle learned of a need for an investigation of the alleged harassment of another employee, Pat.

Most times, the initial report comes from the victim or a witness. Occasionally (rarely), it is the subject of the investigation (i.e., the accused) who provides the initial report. This typically happens when the person is taking responsibility for his/her actions or when someone is trying to preempt the report about his/her behavior by lodging his/her own complaint.

The initial report is most often—but not always—delivered orally. When taking the report, focus on identifying and separating out the facts. Reports often will be delivered bound up with emotions, due in part often because the person doing the reporting believes the reported conduct was inappropriate.

☐ *Understand the emotions and assumptions*

It can be difficult to get to facts if you don't address the emotion first. This may translate into letting someone tell the story how he/she wants to tell it first, then circling back and walking through it for the facts, details, etc. So although we are interested in the facts, primarily, and identifying the emotions for the investigative value, a genuine complainant often first needs to be heard and cared about, before he/she can provide the detailed factual information necessary for the investigation.

First, show you care about the person.

Just because you will have to sift through emotions and assumptions to identify the facts does not make them irrelevant. In fact, you need to identify emotions, assumptions, and initial impressions, as well. You will want to capture all of these in your notes and keep them separate in your investigation file. By separating them out, you are less likely to confuse them with the facts.

☐ *Focus on specifics*

Be sure to focus on specific actions (behaviors and words), not labels. People often use terms incorrectly, particularly trigger words like, "harassment" or "hostile environment" that they have learned through various sources, like a web search. While those might end up being accurate conclusions, you don't know that yet. Use of those words could be unintentional or sensationalism—either way, it can mislead the investigator.

> Note the questions used by Sarah when Walter reported being "cyber-bullied"; these were aimed at trying to identify the specific words or behaviors that led to Walter's conclusion that he was being cyber-bullied.

Additionally, the person reporting the concern has usually had some amount of time to think about how to communicate his/her concern in a way that will get your attention. By obtaining and focusing on descriptions of the specific behaviors and words used, you can separate out what happened or what was said from how it was interpreted. Get the details about the specific behavior and words first and then assess how best to describe or interpret it.

Also, write notes about your first impressions, but keep them separate as well, for later reference. Doing so actually can help later as a means to check yourself to ensure that your investigation did not get tunneled in on the first impressions.

□ **Ensure clear understanding of the complaint**

Once the person feels heard, get the complaint in writing. This will help ensure that the details are captured with clarity. Note that some books on investigations discourage getting written complaints; but, that is based on the presumption that every initial report is true, clear, and complete.

Next, clarify the details of the written complaint. You are looking for exactly what happened, when, where, who, etc. If there has been more than one incident, you need this information about each incident.

> 👁 Chris clarified the details with Wendy using a written question-and-answer format, a useful technique whereby the interviewer writes the question on the original written complaint (using available space on the bottom or back of the sheet or use additional pages) and the complainant answers in writing.

If applicable, you also want to know how the incident has affected the complainant (or victim, if the complainant is not the victim). In your investigation, you should look for terms that are not perfectly clear or generalities that could be more specific (e.g., date, time, location, what happened or was said). Establish whether there is a margin of error on details.

Then assess why certain details are so clear while others are vague (e.g., specific time but the location unclear). This clarity will prevent missteps and aid in your credibility analysis later in the investigation.

> 👁 Chris asked Wendy how she was so certain of the time of the incident with Roger.

Finally, ask the complainant for the names of any persons who he/she told, thinks may have witnessed the encounter, or has other information. Also ask if he/she knows of any relevant documents or other evidence.

☐ ***Make sure nothing was missed***

Once the written complaint is complete and understood, ask the person if there are any other issues that may be relevant or that you should be aware of. It is best to know the full story so the investigator doesn't miss the forest because of the first tree.

Ask the person what he/she feels should be done about the situation. This can help you understand both the situation and the person's mindset better. Clarify that the person is not deciding the organization's response—the organization will assess what it appropriate—but that that you are interested in that person's thoughts.

Close the interview by thanking the person for bringing the information forward, then assess whether there are any safety or retaliation concerns (This will be discussed later in *Address Safety*). Provide a copy of your confidentiality and non-retaliation policies and briefly explain it and inform the person who to contact with any new information or concerns. Reassure the complainant that this matter will be looked into promptly.

△ ***CAUTION: Avoid primacy effect***

Many times, managers, HR, and investigators accept the initial report as completely true. While most complaints are legitimate, they rarely contain a complete—and sometimes, fully accurate—picture of what occurred. Remember that the initial report, even if an honest account of what that person experienced, still represents only one person's perspective of the situation.

△ CAUTION: Don't offer bounties

While you want to encourage reporting, there are significant problems with offering rewards to employees for reporting violations. Some investigators believe this is a way to encourage reporting of small incidents (usually with money offered for any reports) to improve awareness of wrongdoing. However, offering bounties can create two unintended consequences: the creation of a culture of mistrust and an increase in false reporting.

☐ Establish organizational knowledge

Knowing when and how the information came to the organization's attention is important for many reasons. Mainly, an organization is expected to determine the need for an investigation as soon as management learns of potentially illegal conduct. Therefore, you should specifically document who knew what, and when. Recognize that you may find that others knew of the situation prior to the initial report being made. If that is the case, be sure to both ask and document what action was taken, if any.

☐ Reinforce and communicate

Acknowledge and appreciate managers who contact you immediately, because not all do. Don't allow managers to sweep instances (such as substance abuse) under the table, or allow managers or HR to say, "Don't tell me, because if you do, then I have to report/investigate it."

Additionally, communicate who is handling the investigation to managers aware of the situation, even if it commonly understood. This will prevent duplication of effort, unnecessary disruption, and confusion.

Finally, managers need to know what to say if asked by anyone involved in, or curious about, the investigation. The best response is usually to refer him/her to the investigator, HR, or the manager overseeing the investigation.

☐ *Assess purview*

If the case is a police matter, do not interfere with their investigation. Even well-intentioned actions like asking questions can affect this type of investigation negatively.

However, not all government inquiries should be hands off (e.g., a Department of Labor [DOL] wage & hour or an Equal Employment Opportunity Commission [EEOC] investigation). An organization may have an obligation—especially in an EEOC matter—to conduct its own independent investigation.

Additionally, when there is a simultaneous government inquiry, such as an EEOC investigation, the organization should use or coordinate the investigation with an attorney to ensure that witnesses are not unintentionally (or feel as though they are) being influenced on their testimony and to protect your legal interests.

Clear communication and coordination are key during any official investigation. Clearly establish with the respective agency the organization's contact for any questions, assistance, or updates. Also, coordinate in advance any administrative, personnel, or investigative actions that might overlap with the agency's investigation. If you think it should be an official investigation, but the agency you contacted said they would not investigate, it may be worth trying to get an official written notice from that agency.

If an employee of a vendor or service provider is a victim, accused, or witness, coordinate with his/her employing organization. Unfortunately, some organizations mistakenly believe that they have the right to interview anyone in their facilities without hesitation, but then are surprised when a key business relationship falters or fails because of alleged or perceived mistrust. Be sure to consider your contract or service agreement, which may specify the steps that need to be taken with respect to any dispute. Ultimately, you should make a reasonable effort to coordinate the matter with the governing organization without compromising your investigation.

There also may be times to consider the scope of the impact. If the investigation involves areas outside the typical HR expertise and requires the expertise of others (e.g., accounting), get expert input and involvement prior to diving into those records.

☐ *When an investigation may be required*

The duty to investigate may be explicit and implicit in many laws, the most prominent being anti-discrimination laws, Occupational Safety and Health Administration (OSHA), and various state laws.

For example, the EEOC enforcement guide says that an employer is "obligated to investigate [an] allegation [of harassment] regardless of whether [the complaint] conforms to a particular format or is made in writing."[i] Failing to investigate can not only expose an employer to vicarious liability, but also claims of retaliation.

OSHA, which governs worker safety, requires employers to ensure that the workplace is "free from recognized hazards that are causing or likely to cause death or serious physical harm."[ii] To do this, an employer would be required to investigate an obvious safety hazard or complaint of safety violations. (OSHA also has certain recordkeeping requirements, such as the Form 301, which requires you to "investigate" any recordable workplace injury.)

State laws may also mandate an investigation in certain circumstances. Other laws may not explicitly require an investigation, but may offer legal protections for doing so, often in connection with other proactive employer actions.

☐ *Type of investigation*

All investigations involve the gathering of facts and making of credibility determinations via a formal process. However, not all investigations are as exhaustive as others. Although many investigations will be full-blown and extensive, some will be more like an inquiry—not as complex and demanding. Inquiries generally can be focused on understanding and addressing the impacts of the incident(s). Situations that may warrant an inquiry would be when you have a confession already in-hand, or the incident involves less-serious conduct. But an inquiry is still an investigation.

When deciding to investigate, you will need to also decide the extent/type of investigation warranted by the situation (be sure to revisit this decision as the investigation progresses). Consider the seriousness of the conduct, the potential impact/liability, and other relevant factors.

☐ *Assess immediacy*

Initially, recognize that a prompt investigation is desirable for a host of reasons—to enable necessary corrective actions before issues get worse, to ensure the investigation is legally defensible, and for policy reasons—by responding promptly and visibly to a complaint, it builds trust in the complaint process. But given the realities of most workplaces, not all investigations can reasonably be started immediately. As part of the decision to investigate, you should consider the potential impact of any delay in the investigation (starting or completing it). Some situations (e.g., certain safety hazards) must be addressed immediately, whereas others (e.g., petty theft with limited opportunity) could be re-prioritized if needed to accommodate more urgent investigations or activities. A situation that can be reprioritized if necessary is said to have a high delay tolerance, whereas one that must be dealt with immediately has a low delay tolerance.

For any delay that occurs—regardless of a situation's delay tolerance—you should understand and document the reason for any delay and ensure it is not for unacceptable reasons (e.g., schedule convenience, peak business). It also is critical to ensure that you preserve all documents, records, and other evidence until they can be reviewed. Given that many organizations have auto-destruction processes in place or recycle/rewrite over electronic data, failing to take affirmative steps to preserve that evidence could result in the information disappearing or being deleted/disposed. For situations that result in litigation, the loss of evidence could not only impede your ability to conduct a thorough investigation, but also may result in the jury in a resulting trial being instructed that they may presume that the evidence was deleted/destroyed because it was adverse to your organization (adverse inference instruction).

☐ *Get (and stay) organized*

Create a file for all evidence, statements, and notes. In many cases, you may need both an electronic and a paper version of this file. By creating an investigation file, you will be able to readily find and refer to any information needed. Also, it will improve your ability to transition the investigation to someone else if you get called away.

Each investigator develops his/her preference for how the investigative file is organized. For example, the authors of this book create a primary folder (electronic and/or paper) with the investigative plan (including a specific statement about what it is that the investigator is trying to determine), checklists, timeline, notes, etc. Additional folders are created for documents produced and a separate folder is created for each person interviewed.

☐ *See it through*

Part of making a conscious decision to investigate is committing to complete the investigation. This means completing all the steps without taking short-cuts. The steps and phases may vary in duration, but all need to be completed.

Assessing

Decide to investigate

Address safety

Maintain confidentiality

Once you've made the decision to investigate, immediately address the safety of all parties involved.

□ *Complainant and witnesses*

Even with no clear risk of harm, you need to address safety clearly and openly with the complainant. Doing so not only establishes a dialogue with the complainant about safety issues (making it more likely he/she will come to you in the future), but also demonstrates your commitment to remedying harm and reduces the risk of constructive discharge and retaliation claims. Find out if the person has any fears or concerns for physical harm, property damage, retaliation, concerns for getting to/from work, etc. These fears and concerns can involve others not involved in the investigation, including coworkers, friends, or supervisors of the accused. Seek to understand fears that are not clear. With the notification of the complaint, you have been put on notice; failure to address those concerns may result in legal exposure.

Do not put the complainant on personal leave or transfer him/her. Even offering to put the complainant on leave can result in a claim of retaliation, regardless of whether the offer/move is made for safety or out of other protective concern.

Encourage reporting of any concerns to management, the investigator, and—where applicable—the police. Some people hesitate to call the police, assuming that the organization will call if necessary; do not encourage anyone to ignore their intuition if he/she perceives possible danger. Discuss alternatives, such as escorts to/from the car or varying commute routes.

The need to inquire into safety concerns applies to witnesses as well. Witnesses often feel scrutinized and can share many of the same concerns that complainants do.

☐ **The accused**

Options for interim relief may include leave (paid or unpaid) or temporary transfer (of shifts/location) of the accused, telecommuting, a change in reporting relationships, assignment of extra supervision, etc. If you do take interim action in the interest of a complainant, document the action taken and the reasons therefor in your investigative notes. Provide a memo that documents what is happening, why, lists the "ground rules" (e.g., no contact, no destruction of documents), and provides the parties information about whom they can contact with questions or concerns.

Don't forget to address the safety of the accused as well. There could be latent frustration from the complainant, witnesses, or people in management positions in the organization. There also could be loved ones and friends who are protective of the complainant or upset about the allegations, who may be motivated to take matters into their own hands. Everyone involved in the investigation should be instructed to notify management or the investigator if anyone—including family members, friends, or other non-employees—threatens their safety.

☐ *Unknowingly involved*

A less obvious category of people whose safety needs to be considered are those who may be mistakenly blamed. For example, if the complainant's identity is not divulged to the accused, he/she may speculate about the possible source and confront those he/she believes responsible. Those confronted may not have been aware of the incident or investigation.

The primary strategy to prevent putting unknown persons at risk is demonstrating objectivity and fairness to the accused and encouraging him/her to trust the process to bring about a fair resolution. If the accused openly speculates about people, the investigator should not confirm/deny involvement of any person, but again request that the accused trust the process to find the truth. It may help to ask the accused if he/she will let you do that and secure his/her verbal commitment.

☐ *Investigators*

As you take action to address the safety of those involved in the situation, don't forget about your own safety. Even the best-trained and experienced investigators need to be reminded not to put themselves in dangerous situations.

Investigators usually presume they will be respected for their authority and role, which can be a faulty assumption. Investigators should be in-tune with and listen to their intuition. If something seems out-of-sorts, don't ignore those signals; your intuition is a great resource.

Heed your intuition.

In some situations the hostility builds, while in others it seemingly comes out of nowhere. If a witness is hostile but not violent, there are a couple of tactics to try to de-escalate the situation. For example, if the witness is raising his/her voice, lower yours; get quieter and calmer. Suggest taking a short break and inform the witness that the break is to enable him/her to gather his/her thoughts and resume the interview with all emotions in check and exhibiting professional behaviors.

Immediately address any possible concern for safety. Often, the best way to address it is by telling the person you are calling the police, picking up the phone and calling 911. Give your name, location, situation (e.g., "I represent the organization and am conducting an interview with an employee whose behavior makes me concerned about possible workplace violence"), and request police presence. By doing so, the person may calm down and you can cancel the request for support. If not, the police are on the way.

Assessing

Decide to investigate

Address safety

Maintain confidentiality

Many people are reluctant to share their concerns with management. However, if employees and others do not bring situations to your attention to enable you to correct them, those situations negatively impact your organization's productivity, effectiveness, efficiency, and can result in losses—of product, employees, time, and money. How you manage the confidentiality of a concern—once shared with you—directly impacts whether the complainant *and others* will share concerns with you in the future.

☐ *Be trustworthy*

Ideally, your behavior, integrity, and trustworthiness will *build* confidence and actually encourage future reporting.

One key component to building confidence and trust in the system is to avoid overpromising. For example, you should not promise complete secrecy. While you can, and should, assure the complainant that every effort will be made to protect his/her identity, you cannot promise complete secrecy, because in most investigations, doing so would result in a crippled investigation or your breach of that promise. You will need to do your best to assure the complainant that a complete, fair, and confidential (but not totally secret) investigation will be conducted and information will be shared only with those who absolutely need to know. You may have to explain that the consequence of absolute secrecy is an incomplete investigation and without a complete investigation you cannot get an accurate picture of the situation, much less fashion an effective remedy.

The other key component to building confidence and trust is to deliver on your promises. Keep track of things you say you will do and make sure you either do them or let the person know you were not able to. This includes tracking and meeting any timeframes or deadlines.

△ *CAUTION:* **Don't share opinions**

Amazingly, some investigators get comfortable with the complainant, accused, or witnesses and openly speculate about the investigation. Some use it to try to explain others' behavior. Some use it as a lure to make themselves seem more approachable to get the person to open up more. Others just have no grasp of their responsibilities.

This is never acceptable, because it feeds the rumor mill and calls the objectivity of the investigation into question. The appropriate thing to do is listen and ask clarifying questions.

△ *CAUTION:* **Don't deputize witnesses**

If a witness asks the investigator to confirm something that person did not know first-hand (e.g., "I heard that he did ..."), the investigator must politely refuse to answer the question and should address the concern with questions of his/her own ("Why do you think that?" "Where did you hear that?"). Some investigators believe it helps to share a little information, because the person may be able to find out more and report back to the investigator (i.e., a mole); this is unacceptable as it compromises the integrity/reliability of the investigation.

△ *CAUTION: Don't use blanket confidentiality orders*

Whether an investigator is trying to prevent collusion or a manager or HR professional is trying to prevent rumors, blanket confidentiality orders rarely work and they expose the organization to risk. In a 2015 decision, the National Labor Relations Board concluded that blanket confidentiality orders are impermissible and that to impose a confidentiality rule to prevent employees from discussing an investigation, an employer must have a legitimate and substantial business justification that outweighs employees' rights under Section 7 of the National Labor Relations Act to discuss an ongoing disciplinary investigation.[iii] Typically, an employer must be able to articulate specific facts that demonstrate that the integrity of the investigation will be compromised without confidentiality and, to avoid an unfair labor finding, that witnesses need protection, evidence likely will be destroyed, testimony is in danger of being fabricated, a need to prevent a cover-up, and the investigation will be corrupted. Because this presents a fairly high burden and ordinary cases will not meet it, the need for an experienced investigator who can use other available techniques to prevent collusion and protect the integrity of the investigation, is key.

Importantly, the above limitation on the use of confidentiality orders does not apply to management. Indeed, management has the *obligation* to keep things confidential, for among other reasons, to protect the complainant from retaliation. Therefore, confidentiality orders should always be used with management-level employees.

☐ *Remind those involved of confidentiality*

When you have determined that the case permits a request of confidentiality, you want to reduce the likelihood that the complainant (as well as the accused and any witnesses) will discuss the issue with others. Do not miss the opportunity to secure a commitment from the person to keep things confidential.

A good approach is to explain the reasons you are asking for confidentiality (i.e., to enable you to do a full and fair investigation and because people—even very well-intentioned ones—can be influenced by discussions with others). Explain that the need for, and his/her commitment to, confidentiality extends only while the investigation is ongoing and that you will be doing your best to conduct as efficient an investigation as possible. Emphasize the most important thing is to conduct a thorough and accurate investigation and that you will notify him/her once the investigation has concluded.

Most investigators will secure the individual's confidentiality commitment both orally and in writing. This is much more effective in reducing chatter than simply sticking a piece of paper in front of the individual and having him/her sign it. You may also want to specifically ask—immediately prior to the individual signing the acknowledgment—if he/she understands your confidentiality policy and whether he/she has any questions.

Also, clearly state who the person should contact with any new information or any concerns. This will help cut down on confusion, open speculation, and discussions with others. Because the situation is already stressful for the people involved and there will be so many things going through their minds, it is best to have a copy of the organization's policy on confidentiality—even better if it is the one the individual previously signed—and provide it to the person to take away with him/her. You can encourage the individual to write down the contact name and information on bottom or back of his/her copy of the confidentiality policy.

In addition to those being interviewed, other people aware of the investigation need to be reminded of the obligation for confidentiality, including the investigator, those in the supervisory chain, and any manager aware of the investigation. Don't assume that everyone knows the potential impact of sharing information.

Your obligation to ensure confidentiality extends to any confidential documents and the investigative file itself. Mark confidential documents as confidential and restrict access to them. If you must show them to a witness at some point in the investigation, and that witness is in management or you have determined a confidentiality order is justified, remind the witness of his/her commitment to confidentiality before showing him/her (e.g., "I've got a few documents I'd like to ask you about, but before I do, I wanted to remind you of your confidentiality agreement and make sure that you understand that your commitment to confidentiality extends to the information contained on these documents. Do I have that commitment from you?")

And, of course, be sure to secure your confidential investigative file (including the electronic version).

Chapter 2
Michelle Manages Masterfully

It is a short drive from my office to the North site, but it is just long enough to think through the cases the team members are handling. At the stop light, I look in my notepad. We have:

• Wendy vs. Roger at North - harassment
Chris + Tyler handling

• Billy at East - under the influence ✓
Vernon handled

• Walter vs. Keith at South - cyberbully
Sarah handling

• David vs. Sam at South - threats
Lance + Sarah handling

Once I get inside, I'll get an update from Chris on the complaint from Wendy about Roger harassing her. I want to also stay as available as possible to Lance and Sarah as they investigate the verbal threats between David and Sam at the

South Site. Oh! I just remembered that I haven't heard from Tyler about the credit card case at the East site from last week. I'll add that to my list and ask him about it after I get the update from Chris. It will be good that I am here to support Chris, should Tyler need to go to the East site to follow up.

Before I get out of my car, however, my phone rings. It's Lance. "Hello, Lance."

"Hello, Michelle. Well, both Sam and David are getting restless. They are each complaining about the amount of work they need to do and each is saying, 'there's no reason to hold me here; he's the one that was wrong.' So we checked in with each of them, expressed appreciation for their patience and told them that we'll get to the interviews as soon as possible. They are both a bit calmer now. We will definitely need to get witness statements in this one. For expedience, we are going to have Sarah partner with the department manager and they will interview witnesses. John and I will start with interviewing David, while Sam waits in the other office until we can interview him. One thing that I plan on exploring with David is a possible hearing problem, because of the possible misunderstanding of what Sam said."

I interject, "Lance, pardon the interruption, but I don't want to forget this thought. Sarah mentioned to me that she knows both David and Sam, so please check on that."

I can practically hear Lance smiling on the other end of the phone, "Yes. I asked if there are any friendships that may impact the investigation. She said, 'Absolutely not. I just remember each of them from orientation and I did their new hire paperwork, that's all.' Based on that, I don't see any concern regarding her objectivity."

"You're on it, Lance! Please continue."

"So, we checked our schedules and the only potential conflict is that I am scheduled for two days off at the end of this week, on Thursday and Friday. However, we should be able to complete the interviews today and the investigation tomorrow. We have our notes on what John got from David and Sam; however, we will start over and ask to hear everything straight from them. In addition to the standard core questions, we've developed targeted questions for David and Sam, and also for the witnesses."

"Excellent. What are the targeted questions?" I ask.

"The targeted questions for David and Sam are:
- What did you do to try to calm the situation down?
- Do you have any concern working with (the other person)?"

"The targeted questions for the witnesses are:
- Did one or both of them make it worse? How?
- Do you have any concern working around either of them?"

"We've also developed one follow-up question for David, Sam, and the witnesses, in anticipation of pointless blaming of one or the other: 'Does (so & so) being at fault excuse (your/the other party's) behavior that followed?' Sarah will visit the work area in conjunction with the witness interviews. We developed a schedule and planned a break at the same time in both sets of interviews; that way, I will know a little more information before I interview Sam. Fortunately, we have enough private offices for the witnesses, and both Sam and David separately. Sarah will interview those with worksites closest to David and Sam back to back, and I will go to the office where Sam is when I am done interviewing David and meeting with Sarah. Any concerns with the plan?"

I can tell Lance really has a great grasp on investigations. "Great plan, Lance. Please call whenever you need anything."

We hang up as I enter the North site. I head to the conference room and greet Chris and Tyler. Chris greets me and then immediately launches in to an update. "Wendy expressed confidence that we would handle the situation. Because she is friends with Marie and will probably tell her about it, we should keep Marie informed. We also should ask Marie if Wendy had mentioned any concern."

I nod, saying, "Chris, you have a great approach. People trust you to do the right thing and are comfortable around you. Although this is a complex case with low tolerance for error, you have the skills and experience and I am confident with you taking lead on this that we can handle this internally."

Chris' training and experience in investigations have been crucial in so many complex situations. Before I had Chris, I called in an outside investigator for complex cases, particularly allegations of harassment; but her formal training and expertise have enabled us to do more internally. However, Chris can be quite protective of disadvantaged people, so I note that I will need to monitor the case closely to ensure that doesn't influence her objectivity in the investigation.

Chris continues, "Good. I looked at the schedules and time cards and noticed that Roger was not at work on Thursday, the day Wendy said the incident happened. The time cards show that they both worked Monday, which was three days prior and on Friday, which was the day after; however, Pat did not work Monday, so that day won't be as high a priority. The first focus was to check cameras on Thursday at the time Wendy claimed, just in case there is a timecard discrepancy."

Chris turns to Tyler and he chimes in, "First, we confirmed that the system clock was accurate in the surveillance live view. Then, we looked at video, from 30 minutes prior to the window she gave us through 30 minutes after. We did not see Roger at all, which confirms the schedule and time card. Next, we looked at Friday at the time Wendy said, plus 30 minutes prior and 30 minutes after. Nothing was seen; well, the alleged behavior wasn't seen. Even though Wendy was seen at that location during that period, Roger wasn't there during that time. It will require a more thorough inspection of video to see if they were ever there together, which we will do later."

Chris then says, "Tyler, go ahead and tell Michelle what we developed as core questions for the interview." I smile, happy to see Chris' talent extending to the training of someone new. Tyler looks down at a list he created, and says, "The core questions will be:

- How are things in the department?
- Is anyone making things uncomfortable?
- Are you aware of anyone making sexually inappropriate comments? Of inappropriate touching?
- What is the appropriate punishment for someone guilty of this behavior?

- Does someone who is guilty of this behavior deserve a second chance?"

"We also developed targeted questions for Pat and Roger. The targeted questions for Pat will include:

- Did Wendy talk to you about an unusual encounter with another coworker?
- What specifically did Wendy tell you?
- When did she tell you that?
- Did you witness anything?
- Has anyone said anything inappropriate to you or touched you inappropriately?"

"Then, depending on her answers, we will ask:

- How did Wendy act when she told you?
- How do you know when Wendy told you?"

"The targeted questions for Roger are:

- Have you ever said something to a woman at work about her body?
- Have you ever touched a woman at work?"

"If he doesn't understand the targeted questions, we will ask more specifically if he ever told anyone that he liked their breasts and if he ever touched the chest of a woman at work."

Tyler then shoots a side look at Chris and suggests, "I recommend we ask everyone in the department and adjacent departments if Roger has ever said anything inappropriate to them."

From the look Tyler gave Chris and the look on Chris' face now, it appears that they had this discussion and Tyler didn't like the answer Chris gave him. I ask Tyler, "Why?"

Tyler explains, "There may be other concerns that have not yet been brought up."

I ask, "Are there any potential negative effects of this approach?"

Tyler shrugs, "Maybe, but it's worth it."

I persist with, "Let's think through that a bit more. What do you think are the potential concerns of this approach?"

Tyler replies, "Well, it will take time and sometimes people feel unsettled when being placed on the spot or are asked about one or more of their coworkers."

I probe further, "How might that affect the working environment?"

Tyler replies, "Well, it can cause suspicion."

I say, "Right, and it can lead to people speculating about why the question was being asked, causing more discussion about the current investigation, increasing anxiety, and it may unnecessarily strain the working relationships between others and Roger. Additionally, if you apply the logic that there *might* be more out there—which is always true—where do you stop? We can discuss those aspects at the HR staff meeting on Wednesday. For now, we'll focus on the case we have and ask those we interview if there are any other people who should be interviewed."

Chris smiles a knowing smile, then says, "Let's walk the area where Wendy said the incident occurred."

We go to the break room entrance and look around. As we walk, we notice there is also a surveillance camera observing the area around Pat's desk. The three of us head back to the conference room.

Once inside, Tyler says, "I noticed that the door she was using is the only one out of the breakroom, so he may have blocked her path."

Chris acknowledges Tyler's observation then says, "So, the plan is to validate the complaint before we interview Roger. After a more thorough inspection of video, we will first interview Pat. Then we will talk with Wendy again. I'll check with the manager on their schedules." Chris walks next door to the site manager's office and returns moments later. "Pat is planning to leave around 2:00pm, which is in about 30 minutes." Chris sighed, "We still need to look at video. That may take up to an hour. I don't think we should interview anyone until we have reviewed the video and any relevant documentary evidence."

I think for a moment and say, "Okay, we have time to make sure we are thorough. Let's plan to interview them tomorrow while they are at work. What are their schedules tomorrow?"

Chris replies, "Both Pat and Wendy work from 8:00am to 5:00pm. Also, Roger is scheduled on Wednesday from 4:00am until 10:00am. We can use this conference room, which is the same room we interviewed Wendy in. It is private and there is nothing out-of-the-ordinary for people to come here for private discussions of all sorts. There also is plenty of room for us to arrange the chairs so everyone has free access to the exits."

Tyler says, "I think we should also check video to see if Wendy went to talk with Pat after her interview with Chris this morning."

I then say, "Good point, Tyler. Before we continue on this, what is the status on that stolen credit card case at the East site?"

Tyler says, "I'm still waiting on the police to investigate it."

I ask, "What was the last thing they told you? Did they specifically say they were investigating the case?"

Tyler replies, "No, they only said 'thank you' when I gave them the video they requested."

I say, "Okay, because it is not clear, please call the investigating officer and ask if we can proceed with our investigation. When you are done with the call, call me. Chris and I can handle this one."

Tyler packs up his notes, gets up and says, "Will do."

I turn back to Chris as Tyler is leaving, "Do you have the investigation plan drafted up?"

Smiling, Chris says, "I do! I'll have to change it to remove Tyler; will you be supporting me?" as she hands me the draft plan.

"Of course!" I say and read through Chris' plan:

Investigation Plan
RE: Suspected Harassment
Opened July 11, 2016

Issues to be Decided:

Primary Issue #1: Did Roger violate our sexual harassment policy by blocking Wendy in the hallway last Thursday afternoon, and staring at Wendy's chest, telling her he liked her in a suggestive manner, and by touching her breasts?

Primary Issue #2: Did Roger violate our sexual harassment policy by telling Pat he liked her in a suggestive manner, touching her breasts?

Secondary Issue: If Roger violated our sexual harassment policy, what remedial action should be taken?

Members of the Investigative Team (assigned July 11, 2016):

(1) Chris, Assistant Human Resource Director
(2) Tyler, Human Resources Specialist

Summary of Allegations:

Wendy, an employee at Company's North location, complained that the janitor, Roger, blocked her in the doorway exiting the break room on Thursday, July 7, 2016 in the afternoon, between 1:45-2:00pm. Wendy claims that Roger told Wendy he liked her, stared at her chest, used both hands to touch her breasts and said he liked her breasts too. Wendy claims to have immediately reported the incident to her coworker, Pat, who told Wendy that she had something similar happen two days' prior. Wendy made the report to Chris, during a meeting in which Chris was planning on delivering disciplinary action for Wendy's attendance.

p.1

Relevant Policies: (attached)

Employee Handbook: Anti-Harassment Policy, which includes the following applicable text:

Harassment on the basis of race, color, religion, sex, national origin, ancestry, age, disability, genetic information, or other status or characteristic protected by law is a form of discrimination and is prohibited. Harassment can take many forms, including but not limited to:

- *leering, making sexual gestures or mimicking the way someone speaks or moves, or displaying suggestive, or otherwise offensive, objects, pictures, cartoons or posters;*
- *derogatory or offensive remarks, jokes, innuendos, emails, or writings;*
- *making or using derogatory comments, epithets, slurs or sexually explicit jokes about an associate's body or dress; and unwelcome physical contact of a sexual nature.*

If you believe that you are a victim of harassment, or witness what you believe is harassment, you should report it immediately to Human Resources or, if the report involves Human Resources, to the Chief Operating Officer. Reports of discrimination will be investigated promptly, thoroughly and as discreetly as possible. An employee who is determined to have engaged in unlawful discrimination will be subject to discipline, up to and including termination.

Company will not retaliate, or allow retaliation, against any employee or applicant who makes such a report, assists in an investigation of possible discrimination, or files an administrative charge or lawsuit alleging discrimination.

False reports of discrimination also will be investigated and, if an employee is determined to have made such a false report, that employee will be subject to discipline, up to and including termination.

p.2

Potentially Relevant Documents:

Document	Location
Surveillance Video for Thursday afternoon (plus surrounding days) showing: • doorway exiting break room • area surrounding Pat's desk	North security office
Surveillance Video for Monday showing: potential encounters between Wendy & Pat	North security office
Employee Schedules & Time Cards for Last Week	Site manager
Company Employee Handbook, including policies re: retaliation, employee privacy (surveillance) & employee acknowledgements	Human Resources
Training Records for Roger, Wendy & Pat re: sexual harassment & reporting	Human Resources
Personnel files of Roger, Wendy & Pat, including records of any prior claims made or asserted against them; any pending or current disciplinary matters	Human Resources
Supervisor File(s) on Roger, Wendy & Pat	Supervisors
Prior Investigative Files, if any, involving Roger, Wendy, and/or Pat	Human Resources
Emails sent from Company email accounts by Wendy and Pat during past week (Roger doesn't have email)	Information Technology

p.3

Witnesses:

Name	Possible Areas of Knowledge
Wendy (Debra L., Supervisor) North Site	- Encounter with Roger on Thurs - Received report from Pat regarding her prior encounter with Roger of similar sexual nature
Roger (Bill K., Supervisor) North Site	-Allegations re: Incident on Thurs. -Allegations of incident with Pat
Pat (Debra L., Supervisor) North Site	- Incident on Thursday (person to whom incident was initially reported) - Potential second victim of Roger (2 days prior) - Possible contact with complainant immediately following report to Human Resources
Site manager North Site	- Observations of working relationships - Knowledge of any prior complaints - Personal problems with Wendy that may have resulted in Wendy not reporting claim timely
Department managers North Site	- Observations of working relationships - Knowledge of any prior complaints

Types of Investigative Methods to be Employed:

1. Review of video surveillance
2. Review of documentary and electronic evidence
3. Physical inspection of relevant work area
4. Personal Interview with Complainant
5. Personal Interview with Witness, Pat
6. Personal Interview with Accused, Roger

p.4

Risks Present & Mitigating Measures:

Because the Investigative Methods include review of surveillance and review of Company email accounts of employees, to avoid invasion of privacy claims, Human Resources will verify all employees acknowledged copies of our Employee Privacy & Use of Information Technology policies.

Wendy has brought a complaint of hostile work environment (HWE). Both federal and state laws impose liability on Company if this claim is substantiated and remedial action is not promptly taken. Moreover, because this HWE claim could be linked to a prior claim by a coworker and could be claimed to be continuing in nature, there is a risk of (1) a continuing violation, and (2) exposure to punitive damages for failure to monitor/correct if the prior incident was reported (suggesting willful and/or reckless disregard of the employee's rights).

To avoid any potential claim of false imprisonment, any individuals interviewed will be advised that their attendance is voluntary and will be seated closest to the exit door, with no one or thing blocking his/her exit. No threats or physical force will be used to compel an interview.

Investigation Checklist/Steps to Be Taken:

Step	Action	Responsible Party	Estimated Completion
1	Obtain Complaint --Address safety issues --Assess ability to order confidentiality	Chris	Monday
2	Create Plan	Chris	Monday
3	Review Surveillance	Chris/Tyler	Monday

p.5

Step	Action	Responsible Party	Estimated Completion
4	Physical Inspection	Chris/Tyler	Monday
5	Document Review	Chris/Tyler	Monday
6	Interviews with Site & Department Managers	Chris/Tyler	Monday
7	Obtain and Review Time Cards & Schedules – Verify with Roger's supervisor	Chris/Tyler	Monday
8	Prepare timeline	Chris	Monday
9	Prepare all notices & agreements: • Preservation Letter • Witness Notice of Investigation • Witness Agreement Forms	Chris/Tyler	Monday
10	Prepare list of questions for interviews	Chris/Tyler	Monday
11	Set up interviews of Wendy & Pat	Chris	Monday
12	Conduct Interviews of Wendy & Pat & Obtain Witness Statements	Chris/Tyler	Tuesday

p.6

Step	Action	Responsible Party	Estimated Completion
13	Set up interview of Roger	Chris	Tuesday
14	Conduct Interview of Roger & Obtain Witness Statement	Chris/Tyler	Tuesday
15	Collect additional documents	Tyler	Tuesday
16	Update Chronology & Investigative Notes	Chris	Tuesday
17	Conduct follow-up interviews, if necessary	Chris/Tyler	Wednesday
18	Prepare investigative report	Chris	Wednesday

p.7

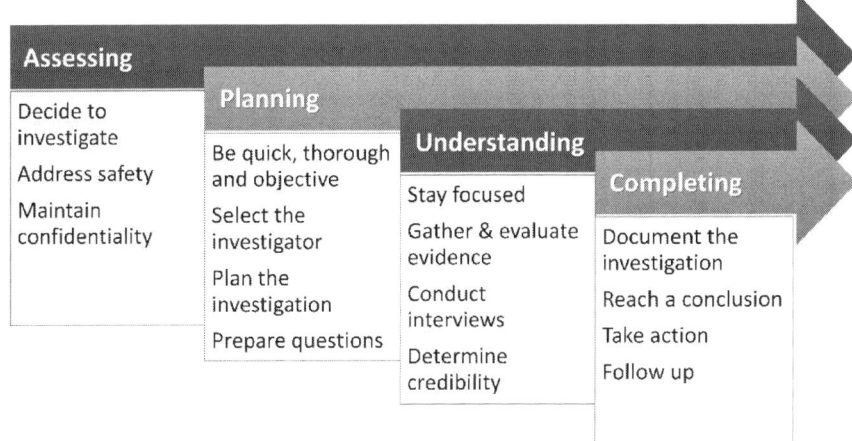

Assessing	Planning	Understanding	Completing
Decide to investigate	Be quick, thorough and objective	Stay focused	Document the investigation
Address safety	Select the investigator	Gather & evaluate evidence	Reach a conclusion
Maintain confidentiality	Plan the investigation	Conduct interviews	Take action
	Prepare questions	Determine credibility	Follow up

Planning

Be quick, thorough and objective

Select the investigator

Plan the investigation

Prepare questions

To be effective, an investigation must begin promptly, must be impartial at all stages, and must be sufficiently thorough or reasonable under the circumstances to be effective at rooting out the complained-of conduct.

☐ *If you're slow, they will go*

If there is delay in initiating or concluding the investigation, the delay may prompt a wary complainant to take the complaint to a government agency or the media, and/or seek legal representation. Other complainants may respond to delay simply by leaving the organization. By acting quickly and keeping the complainant aware of the status, you will have a better chance to complete the investigation and take appropriate action without jeopardizing your employment relationship with the complainant, your business relationships and reputation, and your assets.

Any EEOC investigation, to be defensible, must be prompt, which means that an employer has to launch an investigation immediately after determining one is necessary (which it to happen as soon as management learns of the alleged illegal conduct). Courts have found that "prompt" means within mere days, possibly up to a week; but an investigation delayed by weeks generally is not prompt. By not conducting a prompt investigation, an employer may incur additional liability, and may be exposed to punitive damages if the underlying claim is validated.

☐ *If incomplete, you will have to repeat*

An investigation must be sufficiently thorough or reasonable to root out the complained-of conduct. While each phase and every sub-part of the investigative process requires thoroughness, the evidence and interview steps are the most important. To make a good conclusion, you need to consider all pertinent information. To do that in a timely manner, you must be able to distinguish between what is pertinent and what is not; otherwise, you will waste precious time.

The challenge comes in knowing from the outset what evidence is pertinent. Rejecting something as irrelevant, then later realizing its significance and having to backtrack to relocate that evidence can be disruptive. One method when considering evidence that is not immediately and clearly relevant is to have a tracking sheet that refers to the location and type of information, should it be needed later. This allows you to stay focused on the key information without losing possible leads or spending too much time and effort trying to decide if the information is pertinent. This is particularly necessary with video surveillance, which can consume huge amounts of your time.

When faced with numerous potential witnesses who *may* have some information, recognize that you might not be able to interview every single person. When deciding whom to interview, consider the likelihood of whether he/she knows something not yet revealed, can confirm something that may be counter to other evidence, or can expose a deeper impact of the harm than initially perceived.

For those not interviewed, there may be other issues about which you could have learned had you done the interview. Also consider the impact on the witnesses not interviewed, who may interpret the lack of an interview as a slight, causing that person—and potentially others—to question the objectivity of the investigation. Unfortunately, you won't be able to entirely predict the impact of not interviewing a witness until after the investigation is concluded. If it turns out that the investigation was incomplete, you may have to reopen it and may find it considerably more challenging as you try to overcome the distrust caused by the initial, incomplete investigation.

☐ *If you prejudge, the truth won't budge*

In order to be as objective as possible, you must understand your own biases. Everyone has biases—they are the shortcuts by which we are able to process information rapidly, quickly scanning sets of information and interpreting what we think it means based on our own past experiences. The key is to identify and name our biases so they don't affect our perceptions and decisions unconsciously or indirectly. Some things that commonly affect our perceptions are attire and appearance, language and cultural differences, communication styles and effectiveness, and history of previous complaints.

In order to be fair and objective, we cannot ignore or avoid our biases. Otherwise, we may not realize that the clean-cut person in professional clothing who speaks the same language and has the same cultural background as the investigator, describes his/her story clearly and succinctly, and has never had a complaint made against him/her is not *automatically* more credible than the shaggy person in soiled jeans who primarily speaks another language, was raised elsewhere, is unclear and ineffective with his/her story, or had a couple of previous complaints.

Even more, stereotypes and profiles are rarely helpful, because they can blind you from seeing facts that don't fit that stereotype. Remember, if a model does not predict with 100% certainty, it means the model doesn't always work; therefore, there is risk in presuming the exceptions don't exist or matter. For example, even if an empirical study describes the typical person who violates rules or is violent, it doesn't mean that *all* of the people in that category are violent, and there will be others who do not fit the category who are violent. Without an open mind, the investigator may get tunnel vision, and overlook or dismiss critical evidence.

One other note with respect to impartiality: The obligation to remain impartial applies at all stages of the investigation, from the beginning when the report is taken and the investigator(s) is/are chosen, through the questioning and review of documents. This means that you cannot reach any conclusions about what you believe happened until after review of all reasonably available evidence.

Planning

Be quick, thorough and objective

Select the investigator

Plan the investigation

Prepare questions

Several considerations help ensure the organization uses due diligence through the investigation by selecting the right investigator(s).

☐ *Internal or external?*

Any investigator is likely to be perceived as being biased by those who are dissatisfied by the outcome. This could be because of differing perspectives or even self-preservation (e.g., ego, image).

As objective as the investigator and management believe themselves to be, others may see the situation differently. Internal investigators may feel the effect more acutely, especially in other aspects of their job. For example, an HR professional who tries to build rapport with other departments, handles benefits, and/or conducts leadership development may encounter more resistance and less openness from others after an investigation. However, if the investigation was conducted professionally, this discomfort generally does not last very long and will not be as bad as many may fear.

Because of the flexibility, responsiveness, and cultural awareness, it is worthwhile to consider using an internal investigator, if the organization has that capability. Along with taking less time than an external investigator, typically, there are additional benefits gained from the experience, as the investigator's honed critical thinking skills can be particularly helpful in myriad other business decisions, such as vendor selection, climate assessments, and customer satisfaction. However, if there is a low tolerance for error (e.g., a harassment investigation) or insufficient internal capability, an external investigator may be the better choice.

In certain circumstances, an external investigation is needed, regardless of internal capability. In any investigation of the organization's executives, you should use an outside investigator because of the executive's implicit "control" over any internal employee—an inherent conflict of interest.

If you use an external investigator (e.g., legal counsel or a professional investigator), HR still should be involved. You will need to help get the investigator oriented to the operations and culture of the organization, as well as act as a facilitator and critical thinker—there will be doors to open and new questions to ask as the investigation progresses. Additionally, HR should not miss the opportunity to observe an expert and learn more about the investigative process.

There are several other considerations for deciding to use an external investigator and selecting that investigator. These considerations include the applicability of attorney-client privilege, conversion of your attorney into a witness, cost, experience, and more. Further, you should be aware that investigative reports from third party investigators (external investigators) are subject to the Fair Credit Reporting Act. (More information about selecting an external investigator can be found in the *Appendix*.)

☐ *Key criteria for an internal investigator*

While not all investigations will be within the purview of the
EEOC, their standards are good guidance for the selection of
any investigator (internal or external).

> The employer should ensure that the individual who
> conducts the investigation will objectively gather and
> consider the relevant facts. The alleged harasser should
> not have supervisory authority over the individual who
> conducts the investigation and should not have any
> direct or indirect control over the investigation. Whoever
> conducts the investigation should be well-trained in the
> skills that are required for interviewing witnesses and
> evaluating credibility.[iv]

An internal investigator's training and experience should be
documented in the employee's personnel file. Training (e.g.,
seminars, books [like this one]), and formal training courses in
higher education (e.g., psychology, critical thinking, data
analysis) can further contribute to an investigator's
capabilities. In addition to documenting an investigator's
training, you should track all investigations in which the
person was involved, the type of investigation, and the
individual's specific role.

The investigator's ability to be fair and objective is best
assessed through behavior. If a person has a history and
reputation for being fair and objective (particularly when such
behaviors are documented in performance feedback and review
documents), there is a reasonable expectation that he/she will
be fair and objective in the investigation. However, if the
individual has even minor incidents of preferential treatment or
statements demonstrating bias, you should carefully consider
the person's fitness to conduct the investigation. If the person

does not have much history from which to adequately evaluate his/her fairness and objectivity or the individual is working to develop these traits, it does not necessarily mean that the person cannot serve in an investigative role. There may be a good opportunity to continue that person's development in an investigation with some tolerance for error, partnered with another investigator, and monitored closely by HR leadership.

> For example, in our story Michelle noted the need to oversee Chris' investigation because, although Chris was an experienced investigator, she had a tendency to become protective of disadvantaged persons.

☐ *Additional criteria for an investigator*

Taking the issue of fairness and objectivity to the next level, certain individuals should *not* be the investigator. As stated by the EEOC, the investigator cannot be someone supervised by the accused and should not be supervised by the complainant. This extends well beyond the situation of someone investigating his/her immediate boss, to investigations by anyone within a complainant or accused's chain of supervision.

While there is not the same level of conflict of interest in having an investigator who is the supervisor of an involved person, you should carefully evaluate the influence of past and unrelated encounters, including the perceptions of those encounters. For example, a supervisor who has had concerns with a subordinate's performance issues may not be perceived as objective when the investigation involves that employee as a complainant or accused. Additionally, HR should carefully assess whether the supervisor may have a desire to use the investigation to get rid of an employee whose employment would not otherwise have been terminated.

The investigator should not be someone with an obvious bias (e.g., previously-expressed views on the same/similar situation, personal/financial relationship with any of the parties, or a history of negative incidents with the complainant or accused). There also should not be any friendships or outside relationships that could cause others to question the individual's objectivity.

Finally, not everyone can handle every type of investigation. The investigation may trigger such an emotional response that the person feels he/she needs to champion a cause and make an example of the accused (before actually understanding what happened). While this may be more common in harassment and assault matters, it can also happen with cases such as false reporting or theft from an employer.

Desirable characteristics of an investigator include:

- Open-minded
- Thorough
- Detailed
- Patient
- Trust-worthy
- Credible
- Respected
- Good listener
- Persistent
- Sound judgment
- Curious
- Would make an effective witness

☐ **Continuity of investigator**

While unexpected circumstances may arise, it is important to consider anything foreseeable that may disrupt or delay the investigation. Don't select an investigator who is going on vacation or working on another project that would prevent the investigation from being done quickly and seen all the way through by the investigator selected.

Do not assume that you can merely pass off the investigation to another investigator; avoid doing so unless absolutely necessary. Although there are circumstances where a separate investigator can review the evidence and witness reports from interviews conducted by another and reach a conclusion, it is important to have the same individual(s) conducting all of the witness interviews.

☐ **Number of investigators**

Generally, it is best to have two investigators work together. It helps having someone with whom to collaborate when things are unclear and someone aware of the details with whom to compare notes. It also improves the learning and development of the investigators.

While it may be tempting to divide up the work in order to get it done more quickly, the benefits of the team approach will be lost if the team is fractured. In particular, the most critical time for a second investigator is during the interviews. A study by Driskell & Salas validated several benefits of a second investigator during the interviews, including better questions and understanding of the answers.[v]

In our story, to prevent collusion, Lance and Sarah split up the interviews, enlisting the use of other management during their respective interviews. Importantly, the same investigator interviewed all of the witnesses, and the same investigator interviewed the two parties involved in the altercation.

Having two investigators in the room also reduces the risk of any claims of investigator misconduct that can happen when it is one-on-one in a closed room.

No more than two.

While a third person may be a good opportunity for a person to learn from the primary investigators, any potential benefit is limited and usually outweighed by the increased difficulty in establishing rapport.

When there is only one investigator, include some trusted, neutral person as a witness in the interviews. Exercise caution when asking a manager to be the witness as this may cause a chilling effect and your interview may be less fruitful.

Planning

Be quick, thorough and objective

Select the investigator

Plan the investigation

Prepare questions

A plan is critical for any investigation. It will help you define your objectives, prevent you from going down too many rabbit holes, and help create a written record of the investigation (making the writing of the report much easier). An investigative plan typically includes the following components:

- Summary of the allegations
- Objectives of the investigation
- The names and roles of the investigative team members
- Identification of relevant policies/rules
- List of relevant documents & their possible locations
- List of involved parties and potential witnesses
- Types of investigative methods used
- Identification of any unique risks associated and mitigating measures taken
- Investigative checklist/outline of steps to be taken, in what order, and by whom

☐ *Decide what you are trying to decide*

The first step in developing an investigative plan is to draft a clear, concise statement of what you are trying to determine. In other words, what are the goals/what is the purpose of the investigation? Typically, you will couch the issue to be decided in terms of violation of a workplace policy, practice, or expectation rather than violation of a law.

For example, in the sexual harassment investigation at the North Site, the statement might be framed as a question: "Did Roger violate our sexual harassment policy by blocking Wendy in the hallway last Thursday afternoon, and staring at Wendy's chest, telling her he liked her in a suggestive manner, and by touching her breasts?"

If your investigation will require you to make recommendations as to remedial action, include that as a separate statement.

For example, in the sexual harassment investigation at the North Site, the statement might be framed as another question: "If Roger violated our sexual harassment policy, what remedial action should be taken?"

Whether drafting the issue to be determined as a question or as a simple statement, including it at the very beginning of your investigative plan will help you decide whether evidence (documentary or testamentary) is pertinent (i.e., helps prove or disprove the question) and keep you more focused throughout the investigation.

☐ *Considering the consequences*

In most cases, you should not consider the consequences in the event the accusation proves true. That way, the investigation will be more objective. Indeed, many experts contend that you should split the investigative role from that of making recommendations or taking official action, to avoid the investigator being implicitly influenced by the anticipated role of decision-maker. However, if your organization ultimately plans to bring criminal charges or a civil claim, you will need to account for that in your initial investigative plan. Once you go down certain paths, it removes the opportunity to choose other paths (e.g., if you are counting on a confession, there is no longer the opportunity to catch the person in the act if the conduct is likely to be repeated).

In criminal matters, you should recognize that a higher level of proof will be required, not only for an ultimate conviction, but also to get the police to arrest the perpetrator and the District Attorney (DA) to prosecute the case. The police are juggling more than just your case and will consider your case through the paradigms of what they expect the DA's office will require to prosecute. If they can't envision the DA being willing to prosecute based on the evidence you present to them, the police often will simply refer it to investigators (usually "white collar"), who may or may not do any actual investigating. Even clear video surveillance may not be sufficient to prompt a police investigation. Don't count on a confession alone; the police may determine there is not enough evidence to take the person into custody.

When you plan on bringing a civil lawsuit (e.g., for corporate espionage, or embezzlement), recognize that the investigation will be extremely heavily scrutinized—every choice you make in the investigation, from the witnesses you choose to interview to your choice of words, will be picked apart and examined under a microscope. You should be especially careful here with your preservation and examination of electronic evidence. Ultimately, if you are considering bringing a civil lawsuit, or think you might, you should work with an experienced attorney at the outset of your investigation.

☐ *Identify possible sources of evidence*

When identifying possible sources of evidence, start with:

- All relevant policies, interpretive memos, and acknowledgement forms
- Any prior complaints by or involving the same party, against the accused, or similar in nature, time, or location
- Disciplinary records of both the complainant and the accused
- Items listed of documents obtained from the complainant

Then consider any other non-testamentary evidence that may help you decide the issue before you. This may include video surveillance, emails and other electronic evidence (including that which may have been deleted), text messages, voice mails, pictures, memos, symbols, tangible items, etc. If you are going to do an electronic key-word search, identify the parameters—parties, search terms, etc.—determine from whom you will obtain each item of evidence, who will conduct the relevant search for documents, and whether any expert assistance is necessary to obtain the evidence.

☐ *Witnesses: Selecting whom to interview*

When drafting your initial list of potential witnesses, you will obviously include the person who alerted you to the complaint, and—if not the same party—the alleged victim, as well as the accused. Also consider the list of witnesses provided by the complainant, and add any other potential witnesses who are reasonably expected to have pertinent information (e.g., relevant supervisors and co-workers). These are the persons you must interview, unless—after an interview with the accused—there is no longer any material factual dispute. Note that your list of potential witnesses will likely grow as your investigation proceeds; in fact, you will solicit information from all witnesses about other potential witnesses. Not all witnesses need to be interviewed, as set out in the *If Incomplete, You May Have To Repeat* section, but anyone who is claimed to have direct knowledge of the material disputed incident(s) and anyone identified by both the complainant and accused as having pertinent information must be interviewed.

Other corroborating witnesses or character witnesses may be interviewed depending on the investigation. Consider whether any expert witnesses will be needed (e.g., handwriting experts, forensic computer analysts, auditors). Also consider former employees and third parties who may have pertinent information.

Next to the name of each witness in your investigation file, identify their manager (or company, if a third party), contact information, and a brief summary as to what information you believe he/she may have.

☐ **Investigative methods**

What types of methods of gathering information are you going to use and why? For example, in addition to interviews—the most common—you may conduct physical surveillance or conduct/review electronic surveillance (e.g., cameras, global positioning system [GPS] trackers, tracking software).

Another investigative method is physical inspection. Even if you are familiar with the location, some aspects you may not have previously noticed may help provide context for the incident. Look for surveillance cameras that may have captured the incident or the path to/from that location (both your organization's and possible views from nearby buildings, which you could request). Also look for windows and doors that may have provided someone the opportunity to witness or overhear the incident. Also, orient yourself to the exit(s), and note how many exits and how accessible they are to the location where the incident allegedly occurred. Document the physical inspection with photos, videos, and measurements (as relevant and necessary).

Additional investigative methods to consider—depending on the investigative objective and type of case—are audits, forensic analyses, and undercover operations.

☐ *Risks and mitigating measures*

Every investigation has inherent risks. Your investigative plan should recognize the risks most implicated by the particular set of facts and identify steps you will take to mitigate those risks. Risks can include claims of discrimination arising out the investigative process, invasion of privacy, defamation, false imprisonment (discussed later in *Conduct Interviews*), and retaliation. There also are risks associated with denying employees a representative if requested or requesting an employee take a polygraph—two nuanced issues that require a clear awareness of the law.

A haphazard investigation can result in a discrimination claim. For example, a claim where an employer completes a half-hearted investigation, fails to interview pertinent witnesses, and consequently terminates a male employee for sexual harassment, could invite a claim of discrimination as it leaves open the inference the organization simply concluded that because he was a guy, he must have done it. Fortunately, this is a fairly easy risk to mitigate. Not only should you follow your policies and rely on your training, conduct a full and fair investigation (as detailed in this book), include a statement in your investigative plan that the investigation will proceed in a non-discriminatory manner.

Investigations implicate a host of privacy rights, the contours of which will be governed by applicable law and workplace policy. For example, if your investigation will require search of electronic equipment, the presumption is that you have the right to search an organization's equipment; however, this right is not unlimited and you should check your internal policy statements regarding the existence and scope of any privacy rights associated with the equipment. If the search is of an individual's own personal device, you typically do not have the right to search it absent consent (such as that often given in a bring-your-own device policy/agreement). Your internal policies also should provide guidance in the search of physical property belonging to an individual. Following your policies will help reduce your risk, but those policies should be compliant with the law. For example, although many states and policies may permit the recording of interviews surreptitiously with only the investigator's consent, other states require both parties to consent. Consider also any privacy risks associated with surveillance that will extend outside the workplace.

What about the risk of denying an employee a representative at the investigative meeting? The National Labor Relations Act "guarantees an employee's right to the presence of a union representative at an investigatory interview in which the risk of discipline reasonably inheres" ("Weingarten Rights").[vi] While the National Labor Relations Board (NLRB) currently does not extend this right to non-union employees, recognize that the NLRB has changed its position on the applicability of this right to nonunion employees several times. Investigators should be aware of any potential change, particularly if the NLRB extends Weingarten Rights to non-union employees.

If a person being interviewed asks to bring in a friend or family member for support, ask why. In most cases, the presence of another person will have a negative effect on openness and some information may not come out because of their presence. If the person insists, consider allowing him/her to have someone wait outside and remind him/her that he/she can call a break any time he/she needs to stop (typically, people don't call a break, the person just sits out there without interfering and the problem is solved).

There may be times when there is a legitimate need for support (e.g., a minor, someone with comprehension limitations). In these cases, assess legal requirements first. If there is any flexibility, ask the person being interviewed if he/she wishes to have a support person/parent there during the interview.

☐ *Prepare an investigative checklist*

Included in or with your investigative plan is an investigative checklist. An investigative checklist is a list of steps to take, target dates for the steps, and identification of responsible parties. The checklist may cover actions already taken, such as receipt of the report, assignment of investigator(s), the need for safety/interim relief, and creating the investigative plan. If these have already occurred, you will still include them on your list, identify the date(s) they occurred, the party responsible for accomplishing them, and then check them off as completed.

At this point, several actions remain ahead. You will want to gather and review documents, prepare notices and agreements (e.g., evidence preservation letter, confidentiality agreement), develop questions for interviews, schedule the interviews, conduct any other fact-finding (based on the investigative methods selected), and reach a conclusion as to the factual issue and—if appropriate—make recommendations.

☐ *Scheduling interviews*

If the initial report was not from the alleged victim(s), the victim typically is the next person to interview. However, if the initial report or organizational context is not clear, the next interview should be with a manager who can provide necessary insights.

In most cases, the next person to interview is the accused. If there is more than one suspect, plan to interview the follower(s) (versus leaders or decision-makers) or the more compliant/ respectful one(s) first. If guilty, this is very helpful getting the person to implicate the other or obtaining a confession.

Some investigators prefer to interview some or all witnesses prior to the accused, usually so they are more prepared to confront the accused with all the details.

> That is the case at the North site, where Chris planned to interview Pat before Roger—for the stated intention of validating Wendy's complaint. Recall that Wendy said she had immediately reported her encounter with Roger to Pat.

Interviewing the accused last is a common tactic in theft cases or when you will only get one shot at interviewing the witness. Exercise caution, however, in deciding to interview witnesses before the accused as the risks can often outweigh the benefits. Many times, the accused is aware of the complaint; waiting while others are interviewed will increase tension and could permit destruction of evidence or attempts to influence the investigation. Additionally, it is important to get the accused's perspective while it is fresh, not after it may have been practiced or coached. The investigator can always re-engage with the accused if there are new details to discuss.

Once the accused is interviewed, plan to interview the witnesses. Schedule the interviews at a time that both investigators can be present. If that is not possible without compromising the expediency of the investigation, include a member of management as a witness (primarily for the professionalism of the interview and to prevent any complaints against the interviewer). In cases when neither is appropriate (i.e., privacy is utmost), pay attention to the genders of the investigator and the person being interviewed and avoid a man and a woman alone.

Also, schedule breaks to give the investigator a necessary respite. These will provide the chance to complete the notes from the previous interview while the information is still fresh.

☐ *Language*

Look at the list of individuals to be interviewed and make sure that at least one interviewer will be able to communicate clearly in each individual's native language. If no investigator fits this bill, you will need to provide an interpreter. Failing to use one when a witness does not have a good command of the English language not only is inefficient and ineffective, but also it jeopardizes the legal defensibility of any investigation conducted. If an interpreter is needed (for non-English speakers or the hearing impaired), do not use family or friends of the person being interviewed.

☐ *Location for, and notice of, interviews*

Choose a private room (i.e., no glass doors) that is comfortable (i.e., not a broom closet) and won't be needed by other employees (i.e., not the break room). Ensure that the pathway to and from the interview room is discrete as well. The preferred location will be somewhere with limited visibility of the path of entry and exits. The room should not only be out of view of others, but also out of earshot. Avoid any location that is associated with one party or the other (i.e., their work areas). Be conscious of any possible implicit messages you are sending with the location.

When setting up the interview room, positioning matters. To prevent any claims of false imprisonment, the person being interviewed should have open access to the exit (i.e., the door may be closed for privacy, but there should not be anything blocking their departure). Similarly, there should be open access for the investigators to exit as well, particularly in the event of acute reactions from the person. You can accommodate the need for both to have access to an exit by holding the interview in a conference room or arranging the furniture in such a way that there is not a desk between anyone and the exit (e.g., putting the chairs in a more conversational setting or turning a desk sideways such that all parties have ready access to the exit).

The preferred method of notification will not be out-of-the-ordinary (e.g., not an intercom announcement that "HR wants to see you"). You may want to enlist the assistance of the individual's manager, especially when necessary to secure a spot on the individual's calendar. Have the manager request time for a meeting, meet briefly at the scheduled time, inform the employee of the investigator's desire to interview him/her in connection with a workplace investigation, and have the manager send the individual directly to the interview location.

□ *Preventing collusion*

When there are multiple subjects or witnesses who may collude (i.e., secretly discuss their stories, often to 'get them straight'), consider methods to prevent passing on information. One way is through the scheduling of the interviews, placing a person of concern immediately adjacent to the other person of concern and timing the change so they have less opportunity to collude.

> Word of caution when scheduling interviews at specific times and back-to-back; it is not easy to estimate how long witnesses will take to become comfortable and provide information. Consequently, it is very difficult to give an exact time for the subsequent interview.

Another approach is to have both persons interviewed at the same time, albeit in separate rooms.

> Sarah and Lance prevented collusion by placing David and Sam in separate rooms and the witnesses are going to be interviewed separately in a third room.

△ *CAUTION: No "witch hunts"*

There are cases without a clear suspect, including theft and sabotage. Some investigators take the approach of interviewing lots of people, with the hope of finding discrepancies in statements that can help identify culprits.

The first problem with this approach is that it depends upon a confession, which does not always happen. Second—and more important—lining up and interviewing everyone can foster distrust.

Instead of the witch hunt, the better approach is to develop a plan for targeted interviews with those with the greatest access and review of pertinent evidence. If those do not yield any discrepancies to follow up on, monitor the situation for recurrence or other notable change.

Planning

Be quick, thorough and objective

Select the investigator

Plan the investigation

Prepare questions

Preparing a general list of questions is an essential part of an investigation. In fact, in a court case out of New York, the court found that an investigator's failure to create questions in advance was unreasonable and—together with other deficiencies—resulted in an ineffective investigation.[vii]

☐ *Examine the evidence already obtained*

The evidence will provide insights into existing systems and processes and more clarification may be needed. Additionally, the evidence will help focus the questions on the issue at hand.

△ *CAUTION: Beware interpretations and extraneous material*

See through any interpretations of the initial evidence and focus on the facts themselves. For example, sometimes a reporting manager has already reviewed video surveillance and states what he/she saw, but subsequent review did not show the same interpretation. Another common example is when a reporting manager has added emotion and interpretation to the complainant's report. Moreover, exercise care to focus on facts that are relevant to the issue to be decided or bear on the question of credibility. Avoid focusing on extraneous, unrelated material.

☐ *See the big picture first, then the details*

When preparing questions, move from general to specific. This gives you an opportunity to assess credibility, build rapport, and gauge a witness' willingness to answer questions. This may begin with background questions (e.g., how long he/she has been with the organization, his/her current job), then to determine relationships and perceptions about relevant working conditions, then to the general issues involved, and then to specific and direct (targeted) questions about the particular incidents. If you have to ask embarrassing or unfriendly questions, try to save those for the end as they may cause the witness to become defensive.

Even if you think you know what you are looking for, you don't know everything and you won't know what you don't yet know. The only way to find out is by using open-ended questions. Always ask the what, who, where, when, why, and how questions (although some of the "why" questions should be saved to the end as they can come off as a bit "moralistic" and shut down an interview). Here are some examples to consider:

- What happened? What did you witness? What was said?
- Who did it? Who else may have witnessed it?
- Where did it occur? Where were you when it occurred?
- When did it occur? How long did it last?
- Why did you notice it? Why do you think it happened?
- How did it make you feel?

Keep your questions short and simple, as this increases your chances of a clear, responsive answer. Be straightforward; don't be cute or tricky.

☐ *Develop the core questions*

Specify some questions that you will ask all who are interviewed. These will help to understand the environment/climate of the organization and work group. Some of these questions will be the background questions mentioned above and are good openers, and some will be specific to the incident.

Certain questions can help you understand the culture, explore possible resolution strategies, and may indicate the individual's level of trustworthiness. For instance, toward the end of the interview, you can ask, "What do you feel is appropriate punishment for someone guilty of this behavior?" and/or "Does someone who is guilty of this behavior deserve a second chance?" (Questions regarding consequences will be discussed in more detail in *Conduct Interviews and Determine Credibility*).

Other core questions to ask each witness include:

• Who have you spoken with about this particular issue (and what transpired)?
• Are there any individuals with whom I should speak with about this issue and what information might they have?
• Are there any documents, text messages, emails, or other evidence that you think would be helpful for me to review? (If those documents, pictures, etc., are in the possession of the witness, ask the witness if he/she will provide them to you and arrange a date for the production of the evidence.)
• Is there anything else relevant to this matter that I should know?

☐ *Develop the targeted questions*

There likely will be some questions you don't ask all interviewees, since some witnesses will have observed different aspects and you don't want to inadvertently provide more details or spark their curiosity to find out. Additionally, the accused may be asked unique questions, particularly about intent and circumstances surrounding the key incident(s).

For the investigation to be effective, you must ask the accused about each allegation specifically. After an opportunity to respond to the open-ended who/what/where/when/why/how questions, you will have to ask, outright, "did you do *X*?" You are looking for an unequivocal answer. If the allegation is denied, ask "why do you think someone would say that you did?" Or, "If I had [describe evidence you have], how would you explain that?" If the accused admits the conduct, inquire about his/her awareness of company policy with respect to that conduct.

For witnesses, you may need to ask them about their relationship with the other parties involved (e.g., complainant, accused) and the relationship between the accused and complainant, as applicable.

☐ *Follow-up questions*

One of the best ways to prepare for any follow-up questions during the interview is to consider what might be asked based on certain possible answers to the core and targeted questions.

For example, if a core question is, "What did you observe?", if a witness should reply, "I didn't see anything," a good follow-up might be, "Did you hear anything?" The initial follow-up

questions are usually enough; don't get stuck trying to continue developing all the possible subsequent questions in advance.

Chapter 3
Michelle Mines Morally

Chris says, "Okay. Why would Wendy make a false report?"

I stop her, saying, "Let's not jump to any conclusions yet. Because an initial suspicion of a possible false report from Wendy has already gotten some support, we need to be intent on trying to disprove that hypothesis."

My phone rings; it's Marie. "Hi, Michelle, is there any update on Wendy's complaint?"

I glance at Chris and reply, "We are still reviewing the evidence and will do our interviews tomorrow."

Marie says, "Well, I know Wendy is a good person and want to make sure we are acting on her complaint."

I reply, "I understand," then ask, "Just to confirm, did Wendy ever tell you about being harassed?"

Marie replies, "No, she never mentioned anything like that, which surprises me, because she seems to tell me everything about what is going on at the North site. I wonder if she was too embarrassed to tell me."

"I'll look into that, Marie. I'll call you as soon as we have an update tomorrow morning."

"Okay. Thanks for getting to the bottom of this." Then Marie hangs up.

Chris looks a little dismayed, "Why didn't you tell Marie about our suspicion that Wendy may have made a false report?"

"Because we don't know that to be true and she trusts us to gather the evidence and objectively evaluate it. Remember, we may learn something different a few minutes from now, but Marie won't know the updates. Remind me, what policies did you determine are applicable?"

Chris says, "The employee handbook with the company policies on harassment and false reporting are clear and there is an acknowledgement in all three personnel files. The policies cover, 'unwelcome physical contact of a sexual nature' and 'false reports.' Both are listed as grounds for discipline up to and including immediate termination of employment."

I look at my watch and say, "I need to go back to the office. Please call me when you are done reviewing evidence. Let's plan to meet here tomorrow at 8:00am for the interviews."

Chris says, "Okay," and heads for the video surveillance system.

I get in my car, pull out my notepad, remove Tyler from the harassment investigation and add the credit card caper:

- Wendy vs. Roger at North -
harassment
Chris + Tyler handling
- Billy at East - under the influence ✔
Vernon handled
- Walter vs. Keith at South - cyberbully
Sarah handling
- David vs. Sam at South - threats
Lance + Sarah handling
- Missing credit card at East
Tyler handling

As soon as I start my car, Tyler calls on my phone. "Hi, Michelle. I called the police and they said they are investigating it, but we can do our investigation as well and it won't interfere, so I am going to the East site. I'll check with Vernon to see if he or someone else can be the witness with me for the interviews."

"Good," I say, "please call me with your plan before you start any interviews."

"Okay," Tyler says and we hang up.

I text Lance, "Just checking in on you. Call whenever you are available. Not urgent; at your convenience."

The drive back to the office is another good opportunity to reflect on the cases. Lance and Sarah are interviewing the complainant, accused, and witnesses in parallel for expedience. I wonder if it will be a simple misunderstanding with unnecessary escalation, as Sam indicated. Oh, there's my phone! Lance is calling me already. "Hello, Lance."

"Hello, Michelle. Just an update. Sarah completed two witness interviews and has only one more to go. Those two said the conversation was so quick, they didn't think twice about it. Neither heard what was actually said between David and Sam. They both did say that David sometimes doesn't hear them, so they make sure to get his attention before they speak. They also said David has been a little short–tempered the past month, so they have been walking on eggshells a bit. I finished my interview with David and am about to call in Sam. David admits to telling Sam, 'I'll pound your head' in response to the threat Sam made. When I asked whether he clearly heard the exact words from Sam, he first said he was sure, but he quickly recanted and said it was possible Sam said something else. David brought up that he has been having some trouble hearing, so I have a note to discuss our accommodation policy."

I interrupt, "Great job, Lance. I appreciate that you recognize the additional possible impacts and items to circle back to, but are staying focused on the investigation. Is there anything else before I let you get back to the interviews?"

"No, David is writing his statement and I'll get to Sam right away."

I hang up just as I am pulling into the parking lot. I'll get caught up on things until I hear from Tyler.

After about forty minutes, Tyler calls. "Michelle, is this a good time to discuss my plan?"

"Sure! I'm glad to hear from you."

Tyler says, "Okay, as you recall, the customer notified the police that her credit card had been stolen. She had identified our East site as the likely location for the theft, because she had forgotten her purse in an unused conference room for almost fifteen minutes. She did not notice the card was gone until the next day, so the police had some doubt as to whether our site was actually the point of loss. Although there is no surveillance camera in the conference room, there is a camera around the corner, so I provided the police that video and retained a copy for us. When I reviewed the video with the police, I saw only two people walk in the direction of the conference room during the time window, Henry and Nathan. The police said the card was used at a restaurant that did not have surveillance cameras, so they don't have enough evidence for the case at this time, but they are waiting on the card to be used again. They recommended we proceed with our own investigation."

"So, here's my plan," he continues, "I think the circumstantial evidence that Henry and Nathan were the only people we know were in that area during that time makes them the best place to start."

I interrupt, "But we do not have confirmation that the credit card was taken from our site, correct?"

Tyler says, "True. I am just exploring a possible path."

I ask, "Also, to make sure I understand clearly, isn't there another path to that conference room that was not monitored by surveillance?"

Tyler reassures me, "True. I agree that it is not a sure thing; that's why I have it categorized as circumstantial evidence."

I say, "Good, thanks. Continue describing your plan."

"I've already checked their files and have seen the policy acknowledgements and no record of previous incidents. I'll conduct the interviews and Vernon will support me. There are no known witnesses to interview, so I'll start with Nathan, because he is younger and seems to be more of a follower, and he might want to come clean if given an opportunity. When I'm done with him, I'll interview Henry. Sound good?"

I say hesitantly, "So far, yes, but I need more details. For example, how will you conduct the interviews and what will you ask?"

Tyler says, "Oh, right. Well, I think the direct approach will work best on this one. I'll start with basic questions about their job so I can learn their behavior when telling the truth. When they are comfortable, I'll ask if they know anything about a credit card that was stolen from a purse in that conference room. Really, there's not much to ask, so it will probably be a short interview."

"Well, don't get in a rush, don't pre-judge, and don't use aggressive techniques. Take a break and call me so we can discuss any possible routes to take with the interviews. Also, make sure you pay attention to room setup, and the standard items to discuss—including confidentiality, retaliation, and who to contact."

Tyler says, "Absolutely! I have a great folder set up with all of the pieces I need and I'm ready to conduct a good investigation."

"Great," I say, "Call me when you take a break."

"Will do," Tyler says and we hang up.

A while later, Chris calls with her update, "Along with Roger's previous discipline for being argumentative with the other department's manager and the site manager, there is a note regarding two separate verbal counseling sessions for not following instructions. Wendy has numerous notes regarding verbal counseling and two written disciplinary records for being late. And, of course, there is the counseling on lateness that was supposed to be delivered Monday when she made the allegations against Roger. Pat has no negative documentation. There are no previous investigation files on any of the people involved. There are no unofficial files that either supervisor keeps; they both have very good filing systems. There are also no emails or other records related to the incident or the people involved. When talking with Roger's supervisor, I verified the time card records. I was able to confirm that Roger was not working Wednesday or Thursday. The video system is functioning normally. It is retaining 35 days of recordings and the clock is accurate. I first looked to see if Wendy went to Pat's desk after the interview, and sure enough, she went straight to Pat's desk and they talked for exactly four minutes and 18 seconds, so I added questions about that meeting to both Pat's and Wendy's lists of interview questions. I fast-forwarded the video to see if Wendy came back to Pat's desk. I saw her just once more, but it was just a short conversation in passing. I saved that and both pertinent views we had already reviewed from Friday, the day after the alleged incident with Roger."

I say, "Well done, Chris. Have you made a timeline yet?" Chris says, "Yes, and I just scanned and sent it to your email, so you should have it already."

I check my email and see the message from Chris. "Great! I'll look at it and then I'll see you tomorrow at 8:00am at the North site."

"Okay. I'll stay here until I am done for the day. Talk to you later." We hang up and I look at the timeline:

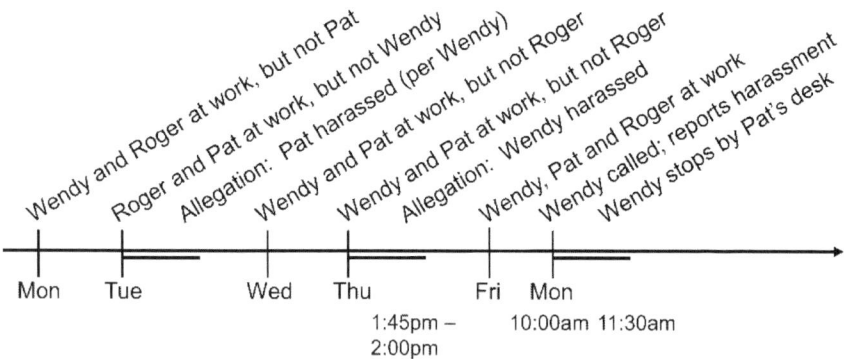

As I'm studying the timeline, Lance calls. "Well, that was interesting!" He sounds a little shaken.

"Lance, are you okay?" I ask.

"Yes, everything is fine now, but the path wasn't smooth. I knew Sam was getting upset, so John and I were planning on using verbal judo to get him focused if he got defensive, which happened right away. Sam said David 'was in my face,' so I asked Sam to stand up and show me, and he got right in my face. I asked if he could show me in the work area, since almost everyone was gone for the day, so the three of us went out there. This time, when Sam walked through it, there was more space than I would have pictured from his description or the demonstration in the office. While we were out there, I simply said, 'thank you' and we returned to the office."

"Once we were seated, I asked Sam if he recognized the difference between his words, the first demonstration, and the walk-through in the work area. He stood up abruptly, his face turned red and he said we were ganging up on him and letting David run the show. I calmly asked him to sit down, which didn't get a response. John told Sam to sit down, which also did not get a response. John told him again, more sternly, 'Sit down.' Sam got louder, pointing his finger at John and accusing him of being unfair and intolerant. I told Sam if he didn't sit down, I would call the police (while I was picking up the phone). Sam paused, exhaled and sat down, so I put down the phone. He asked if I would have called the police and I replied, 'Yes. I would have told them we have an aggressive employee and I am concerned for my safety.' Sam took a deep breath and apologized. I explained to Sam that we are just trying to understand his side of the story. I asked Sam if he wanted to continue the discussion today or come back to talk tomorrow. He apologized again and said he would like to talk now. We finished the interview, which ended up matching everything Sam had reported earlier and what David reported."

"The third witness who Sarah interviewed did not hear what was said today between David and Sam, but he did comment that both of them could be a bit more tolerant of each other. Oh, and Sarah did ask each of the witnesses whether David and Sam joke around, just in case it was a misunderstanding or a joke gone wrong, and they all said that David and Sam are straightforward and don't joke around much."

I interject, "Well, Lance, I am glad you handled the situation so well. That will be an important thing to share at the HR meeting on Wednesday; I never want to miss an opportunity to reinforce listening to our intuition. Are you done for the day?"

Lance says, "Almost. John and I are comparing notes and we plan to sit down with both David and Sam tomorrow morning. We'll have Sarah here for that, too."

I say, "Good plan. Call me if you need anything," and I hang up the phone. Along with catching up on other tasks and issues, I listen to the voicemails from Chris this morning. All very clear, short, and to the point. She is very good.

After almost an hour, it is 6:00pm and I haven't heard from Tyler. I call his number, but there is no answer. I leave a message, "Tyler, just looking for an update. Call when you are available."

Well, I can take his call from anywhere, so I'll head home. And, sure enough, a little later, my phone rings and Tyler says, "Sorry I couldn't answer the phone when you called a little while ago. We were just about to get the second confession and I didn't want to lose the momentum."

I smile, "Really? You got two confessions. Well done. In writing and everything?"

"Oh yeah, it's in writing. So, do you want them terminated?" Tyler asks.

"No. There's no need to rush. Let me review the case and the confessions first. Just tell them they are suspended without pay, pending completion of the investigation. Give them the information on the employee assistance program. When will I see the report?"

Tyler thinks for a moment and says, "I can get it to you by noon tomorrow; is that okay?"

I say, "Yes, that will be good. Tell the two employees to contact Vernon tomorrow at 4:00pm and let Vernon know that I'll call him after reviewing the report, so he'll know what to tell them."

Tyler says, "okay," and hangs up. I nod with satisfaction and say to the drivers all around (who can't hear me through the closed windows), "Tyler was a good hire, alright." As the drivers around me pay no attention, the phone vibrates to notify me of another incoming call.

Sarah says, "Well, I guess Walter's dad is not happy with the way I handled the cyber-bullying case earlier today at the South site. His dad called John, the site manager, and demanded information about the case. John did a great job and simply told Walter's dad that he appreciated his concern, but needed to respect the privacy of those involved and could not divulge anything to him. John said that the dad threatened to sue us and demanded the information. John stated that it was against company policy and if he has any concerns that he should contact HR and gave him the office number. I wouldn't be surprised if I have an interesting voicemail by tomorrow morning! If so, I'll call him with the same response. After all, we don't actually know who is on the phone."

I beam with pride. She's great! "Thanks, Sarah."

And, almost like there was no break at all, it's the next morning and I re-check my notepad:

- Wendy vs. Roger at North - harassment
  Chris + Tyler handling
- Billy at East - under the influence ✓
  Vernon handled
- Walter vs. Keith at South - cyberbully ✓
  Sarah handling
- David vs. Sam at South - threats
  Lance + Sarah handling
- Missing credit card at East
  Tyler handling
  Henry and Nathan

Not much later, I am driving to the North site to support Chris. When I get there, I find Chris in the room examining the investigation folder.

"That was a good timeline you sent last night, Chris. Please plan to show that at the HR staff meeting tomorrow. So, today you'll do the interview and I'll witness. Like we've done before, just ask me if there is anything else when you are done with the questioning and ready to conclude the interview. When everything is done, I will follow Pat back to her desk and linger until Wendy has passed, in order to prevent collusion."

Chris calls Pat on the phone and asks her to come to that office.

Pat arrives moments later. "Hello, Pat. I'm Chris from HR. I don't think we've met."

Pat is a little hesitant, probably because she doesn't know why she was called here. "Hi, Chris."

I chime in, "Hello, Pat, good to see you again."

Pat isn't relaxed. "You, too, Michelle. What's up?"

Chris speaks up, "We're hoping you can help us understand something we heard about."

Pat's demeanor changes abruptly to be very confident. "Yeah, you mean Roger and the way he touched Wendy and the things he said to her."

Chris asks, "Do you know something about that?"

Pat says, "Yes, Michelle came right to me on Thursday at 1:50pm and told me that Roger had just groped her. She was very upset."

Chris asks, "Did you witness it?"

Pat shakes her head slightly, "No, but I believe Wendy. She was really upset."

Chris acknowledges, "That type of incident would be upsetting." She gets more details from Pat about what Wendy said specifically about what happened and then asks, "Have you ever had any problems with Roger?"

Pat looks to the ground, "Oh, he's okay."

Chris asks, "Has he ever said or done things that made you uncomfortable?"

Pat looks up to face Chris, "Well, he's different, you know. No, he hasn't done or said anything that I can think of. Not really."

Chris makes sure her tone is compassionate and concerned, "Has he ever said he likes you, talked about your body, or touched you inappropriately?"

"No, not that I recall." As I keep track of her behaviors, I write in my notes next to the discussion topic, "(Pat is looking at her fingernails instead of at Chris.)"

Chris asks, "You seem uncomfortable, Pat"

Pat says, "A little. I just don't know anything specific."

Chris says, "Okay, well if anything comes to mind, let us know, because we can help."

Pat says, "Okay."

Chris refers to her notes as she continues, "So, you said that Michelle came to you on Thursday and she was upset when she told you about Roger's actions; is that correct?"

Pat looks straight at Chris, "Yes."

Chris says, "I'm concerned. Since that is now five days ago, why didn't you tell the manager?"

Pat says, "Well, Wendy said that she could deal with it and just wanted to get it off her chest and that she would be fine."

Chris asks, "Did you think Roger's conduct was a problem?"

Pat gives an incredulous look and says, "Yes, it is inappropriate. Roger has a wife and he is stronger than Wendy."

Chris says, "Well, if you understand that type of conduct is a problem, do you understand why we need you to report it? We care and we want to make sure that we take care of our people."

Pat says, "I understand."

Chris doesn't pause and asks, "A different question. How sure are you of the date and time that Wendy came to you?"

Pat looks smug, "Very sure."

Chris looks back through her notes, "The reason I ask is because I can't find anything on video at that time and I am wondering if it is possible that it was on a different date or time."

Pat gives a look of surprise, but it seems forced, "No, I'm sure, because it was right before the Thursday weekly teleconference I had to dial into at 2:00pm, which was 10 minutes after that."

Chris sounds as if she accepts that explanation and says, "I see. And Wendy told you at that time that the encounter with Roger just happened?"

Pat says, "Yes, immediately prior to that."

Chris is writing notes and says, "Good, that helps. And did you talk to Wendy yesterday?"

Pat looks to her fingernails but then quickly back up to look at Chris' face, "We said hi when we came in, but I didn't see her the rest of the day. I left early yesterday."

Chris says, "Okay. Let me go back to the day that Wendy told you about the issue with Roger. Not only can't I find anything on video, but Roger was not at work that day at all. Please help me understand that."

I write in my notes, "(Pat maintains eye contact, but her legs, which were moving restlessly before, are still)".

Pat speaks a little more slowly, "Really? I am sure it was that day. Maybe it was the day before?"

Chris pauses thoughtfully, nods, and writes a note while saying, "Okay. We'll check the day before also ... well, actually," Chris opens the folder, shielding it from Pat's view (I note that Pat's lips are now pursed), and flips to Roger's time sheet, "hmmmm, Roger didn't work that day either." Chris shakes her head a little, shrugs her shoulders in a dismissive way, and says, "Let's go back to yesterday. I also know you and Wendy talked yesterday at 11:35am. What did you talk about?"

Pat says, "Nothing; I didn't see her since we came in."

Chris says, "Pat, I know you talked to her because I see it on camera. In fact, I know it lasted for four minutes and 18 seconds. What did you discuss?"

Pat says, "Oh, that?"

Pat says, "Listen, I don't want to discuss this anymore. I am really uncomfortable."

Chris sits back and says calmly, "Okay, I won't keep you here. Do you mind if I ask another question?"

I note, "(Chris made it clear Pat is free to leave and asked if she could ask another question. Pat stayed in place and fixed her gaze on me for a moment.)".

Chris asks, "What do you think should be done if Roger did the things Wendy said happened?"

Pat says, "Well, he should be told to stop."

Chris asks, "So, do you mean given a verbal counseling? Are you aware of what the company policy is for behavior like that?"

Pat says softly, "Yes, termination."

Chris asks, "So, you are aware of the company's policy to not tolerate sexual harassment?"

Pat says, "Yes."

Chris asks, "And so, you understand that, if we believe the events you have told us about, we would terminate Roger's employment?"

Pat looks at her fingernails and says, "Maybe, yes."

Chris asks, "And are you comfortable that your statement would have helped make that happen?"

Pat says, "Well, no," and tears start down her face.

Chris hands her a tissue, and waits. After a moment or two of silence with only Pat's occasional sob or sniffle, Pat blurts out, "I was just trying to help out a friend. I didn't want to hurt Roger or anything, I just figured he would be told to stop and we could go on with life."

Chris says, "But, you've already told me that you know that the consequence of sexual harassment is termination." She stops to see if Pat will offer any further explanation.

Pat stands up and sobs, "I'm leaving."

Chris says, "We're just asking a few questions."

Pat repeats, "I'm leaving." She pauses, staring toward the far wall. After just a few seconds, she looks down to the floor and says, "I just wanted to help Wendy, that's all. Roger is creepy," Pat turns back to face us, "and I thought you would have him keep to himself better."

Chris asks, "Would you like to sit down and continue talking?"

Pat looks to the door, then looks back at Chris and says, "I was ready to leave in a couple months anyway, so I'll just quit now."

Chris says, "There's no need to quit; I'd like to understand more of what has been going on."

Pat gives a sarcastic chuckle and says, "You won't get any more from me. I quit."

Chris says, "We have free counseling with our employee assistance program; here is the number." Chris hands her a business card we have prepared for just such scenarios. "Also, call HR at the office if you have any further questions. Are you willing to write your resignation for me?"

Pat replies, "No."

Chris says, "Okay, we accept your resignation. Would you like a moment to collect yourself?"

Pat opens the door and says, "No, I'm fine. I just want to leave."

As I stand up and move to follow Pat, Chris says, "Okay, Michelle will walk with you." I follow Pat down the hall to her desk where she grabs her purse, keys, and personal effects, and then I follow her out of the building.

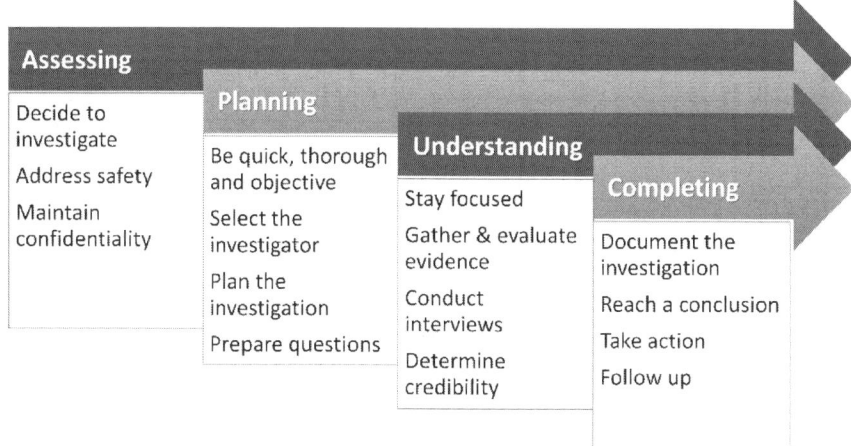

Understanding

Stay focused

Gather & evaluate evidence

Conduct interviews

Determine credibility

It is important to stay focused throughout the investigation. Although it is not a "step" in the sense of a specific action, staying focused can begin to become more elusive as you implement your plan. Use this opportunity to put measures in place to periodically check whether you are staying focused through the rest of the investigation.

☐ *Truth is the purpose*

The purpose of the investigation is to find the truth. Amazingly, some books on investigations infer or directly state that the goal is to prove guilt—they are wrong. Unfortunately, some investigators have accepted that incorrect advice. Also, some over-zealous investigators are looking for a 'catch' as a measure of success. This perspective is often related to emotional issues, can cloud judgement, and results in guilt being attributed to innocent people, while the actual guilty party gets away with deceiving the investigator and the organization.

The purpose is to find the truth.

One way to set the stage properly is to keep the principle of 'innocent until proven guilty' in mind. Even better, when an investigator has a hypothesis, he/she should seek to disprove it. Otherwise, many investigators spend their time and effort validating initial assumptions, which could have been false.

Seek to disprove your hypothesis.

□ Motive

As interesting and exciting as motive can be, it can mislead investigators to interpret information in a manner consistent with the purported motive and lead to investigators screening out information necessary to the investigation. There may be times that a certain person becomes a suspect due to known/suspected issues (e.g., jealousy over promotion, spurned lover, retaliation for a complaint), whereby the actual culprit was not even considered because the focus went to the first person.

When stuck on the motive, many investigators ask, "Why would he/she do that?" The real answer may be that you won't be able to understand it because of different values, paradigms or mental models, even to the point of dealing with narcissists and sociopaths.

Don't get stuck on the motive.

Joseph Burgo estimates 5% of the population are extreme narcissists (which come from all walks of life),[viii] and Martha Stout estimates 4% of the population are sociopathic.[ix] Narcissists are interpersonally exploitative and lack empathy, while sociopaths are without conscience. Unfortunately, most people are simply unable to recognize when they are dealing with a narcissist or sociopath.

This is not to say that motive is entirely irrelevant. For example, in cases of financial impropriety or other instances of fraud, a person's incentive or motive (along with opportunity and rationalization) is very relevant. However, investigators must recognize that motive can come in many forms.

To avoid the question of motive tainting an investigation, you should wait to inquire about motive until you have gathered and analyzed all objective facts.

In the investigation at the East side into the credit card theft, Tyler would not have looked into whether Henry and/or Nathan had financial difficulties until having reviewed surveillance video and questioned them about the unattended purse and missing credit card.

Another benefit of waiting until the end of an interview to inquire about motive is that you may be inquiring about the motive of another. For example, a witness may vehemently defend an accused. In that case, you may want to ask, "why would anyone say that [the accused] [took the action complained-of]."

□ *Supervisors & chain of command*

Many supervisors—particularly those who have never been trained or had much experience with investigations—have a tendency to give more credence to primacy and halo effects (described in *Some Common Threats to Critical Thinking* in the *Appendix*), either believing the first report as completely true or rejecting the first report because, "I don't see the accused doing this."

Even more troubling are those who seek a quick solution, making an employment or disciplinary decision before the facts are known. Whether avoiding the effort or the care to be fair and objective, it can just make things worse in the long run.

It is important to keep affected supervisors—particularly those in the immediate work area—informed on the status of the investigation as it progresses. If you try to keep it completely secret, tension may increase and trust may decrease. However, you don't want to give too much information, particularly anything that is incomplete or speculative. While the investigator has the opportunity to dig deeper and reach conclusions of validity, anyone outside the investigative process may use that unperfected information to make decisions or discuss with others (e.g., their boss). This may taint your investigation and result in incorrect judgments that affect others.

Recall how Michelle handled Marie's inquiry into the situation with Wendy. Although Chris and Michelle suspected a false report, it still was just a theory. Michelle gave a procedural update on the investigation and used the opportunity to informally question Marie whether Wendy had ever reported any harassment to her.

Don't promise to keep all supervisors updated; that can unnecessarily delay the investigation. But telling specific people when to expect updates will keep them calmer and give the investigator more room to stay focused.

☐ *Friends and family*

Often, people who care about those involved in the investigation want to be helpful and may contact the investigator or HR, demanding information. In most cases, the primary concern is maintaining privacy. This means that the appropriate answer is usually, "I appreciate your concern; however, I need to respect his/her privacy and cannot discuss this investigation with you." Most of the time, people understand and accept that. If not, they may threaten legal action, etc., but that should not divert you from doing the right thing and not discussing the case.

Respect and protect privacy.

Like any other threat of legal action, you should notify your legal counsel and, as applicable, your insurance carrier.

☐ *Investigator*

Some investigators ignore evidence because they cannot imagine why anyone would do the alleged behavior (e.g., the action being investigated or why the complainant would ever falsely accuse someone). The problem here is motive or intent getting in the way of the facts. It is critical that the investigator does not get distracted or misled trying to project his/her own values into the investigation.

Sometimes, the investigator can become disturbed by the situation. Even if the investigator has dealt with similar incidents before, there can be elements or factors that cause an emotional reaction. HR needs to be prepared to support the investigator and even change the investigator if the investigator's objectivity is called into question.

☐ *When things vary from the plan*

No doubt about it, things will vary from your plan. Generally, investigators need to follow wherever the evidence leads; however, it should not be done blindly. There should be an assessment—with HR management involved—to decide the priorities and timelines. There may be unexpected twists,

---

👁 While investigating the situation with Sam and David at the South Site, Lance learned that David may be suffering from hearing problems, implicating the organization's reasonable accommodation policy. Lance noted the need to address with David—outside the investigative interview—whether he may qualify for and benefit from the accommodation policy and process.

---

deeper or broader impact, additional allegations, etc., that could not have been predicted when the plan was developed.

If the focus of your investigation broadens as evidence of a larger problem comes to light, make that decision intentionally (i.e., not because an interview turned into a general "gripe" session).

Sometimes, the plan needs to be modified to accommodate a witness' availability (e.g., a person not available to interview at the scheduled time) or if other urgent circumstances arise. Assess the reason for the delay (also determine if it is legitimate) and the potential negative impact on the investigation before agreeing to the change. If the change is acceptable, confirm the new plan, then assess how to best use the time that is now available.

Understanding

Stay focused

Gather & evaluate evidence

Conduct interviews

Determine credibility

Some books on investigations have the interviews prior to gathering documentary, electronic, and tangible evidence, explaining that the information from the interviews will help focus the research of documents. The most effective interviews are those in which documentary, electronic, and tangible evidence are used in the drafting of questions and, at times, the witness is provided the opportunity to offer an explanation. Therefore, it is best to gather this evidence prior to conducting interviews and then obtain any additional evidence revealed during the interviews. For example, if investigating an allegation of timecard fraud, it is far better to have the timecard history and have reviewed available video prior to creating a stir with potential witnesses and unsettling the subject, particularly if the allegation is unfounded.

☐ *Refer to policy and law*

Even if it is already known and understood, the best place to start is with existing policies and, to the extent relevant, the law. Typically, you will do this as you formulate your investigative plan and articulate your objective, but you should frequently return to the standards set forth in the policies/law. The details help discern the specific alleged offense. It also provides the framework for the questions the investigator needs to answer (i.e., did a person violate *X* policy by doing *Y* action?). This will also help identify any previous cases that may establish precedence and cultural norms that may be involved.

□ *Records*

Review the list of documents identified in your investigative report and begin pulling those you believe are pertinent. Keep track of all documents reviewed, both as a record for your investigative report and to refer to later if needed.

Be sure to review the personnel files (both electronic and paper) of the people involved; the main things you are looking for here are policy acknowledgements and previous discipline. Then examine previous investigation files for any involvement as well. In most organizations, you're not done yet. Many supervisors maintain unofficial files as well, so you need to check with the supervisors of those involved to review any documents not in the file, including any supervisor notes.

There will be other records to gather, including time cards, productivity reports, memos, emails and order forms. Note the dates on the record and on the electronic file, when applicable.

□ *Searches of persons and property*

If your investigative methods include physical searches, be sure to implement any mitigating measures you've previously identified—including strict adherence to the organization's policy that specifies what locations and items may be searched (presuming the policy is compliant with the law). Typical locations are employee lockers, desks and other organization property that the employee uses to perform his/her job.

Again, dependent on the organization's policy giving advance notice to employees that they may be subject to such searches, some situations warrant asking the employee to open a bag, purse, backpack, outer-garment or turn out their pockets.

△ CAUTION: Searches must be limited

Investigators and managers should never open, reach into or examine personnel and their property (e.g., purses) themselves, even with permission. In particular, never search an employee's person (e.g., frisk, pat down).

□ Electronic searches

As with physical searches, your searches of electronic devices should be done consistent with all mitigating measures identified and company policy. If support is needed from Information Technology (IT), clearly brief them on confidentiality and get written acknowledgement. It is best to describe what you are looking for, because they will understand better how to find it and what other evidence might be available. You may need to provide to IT the names and persons whose electronic files are to be searched, key words, and dates to guide the search.

The best way to get evidence from private electronic sources is with a written consent and release from one of the parties. As noted previously, if the person was using his/her personal device under a Bring Your Own Device (BYOD) policy, consent may have been given in the BYOD agreement. If consent was not given in advance, you should not expect to get consent where the accused allegedly committed the workplace violation using the device or the device is storing the "smoking gun" evidence. For example, if an employee complains about threatening text or email messages, it is not helpful to confront the accused and expect him/her to sign a release to search his/her personal electronic device until you have the evidence in-hand (e.g., from the other party to the investigation).

☐ *Video surveillance*

Before diving into video surveillance, thoroughly orient yourself to the cameras' location and views. Next, check the clock on the system in the live view and write a note about any difference from actual time. This is critical to finding events when people said they happened and explaining oddities in case of a lawsuit or government involvement.

One effective approach when reviewing video surveillance is to fast forward the video, looking for pattern changes. When a change is noticed, study the video in real time and note the on-screen date and

Search video in fast forward first.

time of the change. Along with the activity during the change in behavior, look at the activity before and after the behavior change. If anything is seen, note the camera designation, on-screen date and time and what was seen in the investigation notes. It may not be clear now, but there may be something worth examining further.

> Example: Three managers had spent a few hours watching video, trying to see the dollar bills that were missing. They called the investigator to come help, saying they had not seen any money visible.
>
> The investigator used the fast forward function, focusing on the employee's behavior. The investigator noticed the employee had put on his jacket (for no obvious reason), walked in a small circle (seemingly to check the door and window prior to reaching into the enclosed area), kept his arm in the enclosed area for a while, then pulled his arm out with his hand cupped at the end of his cuff. Focusing on behavior and watching on fast forward identified key information in less than fifteen minutes.

Before finishing up, save copies of the video and include views from nearby cameras or those on the way to/from the location of the incident. It also helps to get a few minutes before and after any events, in case there is other activity that may be related.

Save video before it's gone.

In many cases, the video footage ends up being a lead that can help find other evidence or focus the interviews. Even if it does not prove anything, it is very helpful in the investigation.

△ **CAUTION: Control video access**

Limit access to the surveillance system. When employees are aware of camera views, they sometimes capitalize on the gaps in coverage. Limiting access also will reduce the inadvertent erasing/overwriting that can destroy the most useful evidence.

There also are well-intentioned managers who will spend far too much time watching video. Even if it is for good reasons, it takes them away from their primary responsibilities and the footage they are seeking usually can wait for an investigator or HR.

Finally, the best approach is to not release video without a very good reason. Generally, good reasons include cooperating with a request from (a) the police, or (b) a government agency, or responding to a court order.

When the accused is not cooperating or demands to see the video, it is sometimes helpful to show the video, if it clearly shows something significant. It might assist in getting a confession, because the investigator gets to watch the person's reaction. However, if it is not clear (i.e., it requires you to interpret what is happening or to infer facts from what is observed), it can bolster the person's claims that the video doesn't show anything or that it is being misinterpreted. The best response to "I want to see the video" is usually, "We'll get to that" and then wait until all questions have been exhausted first.

Some organizations release video to complainants or victims; this is a bad idea for many reasons. There is possible identifying information (e.g., physical descriptions, license plates) and you do not know what the person might do with the information. If someone wants access to video, explain that it is against policy and that you would willingly cooperate with police.

☐ *Develop a timeline*

Capture key events—including the notification to the organization—on a simple timeline. This tool is particularly helpful when connecting the pieces from various sources. Differentiate facts from assumptions, but include both on the timeline.

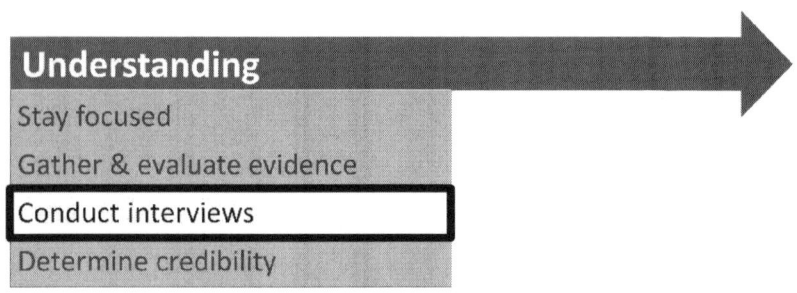

Understanding
Stay focused
Gather & evaluate evidence
Conduct interviews
Determine credibility

Interviews are serious and important business affairs. Behaviors such as joking, sarcasm, eye-rolling, or threats do not belong. This often is easier for the primary interviewer to remember, but is critical for the second interviewer (or manager) as well. It may be difficult, but refrain from reacting emotionally to what the witness is saying—you should be the model of professionalism and open-mindedness. This does not mean that you should be a robot and cannot be empathetic, etc., but you cannot let yourself become emotionally drawn in. Emotions, such as anger, will cause you to lose control of the interview.

Consider how your words and behavior are perceived.

☐ **Set the stage**

When the person arrives for the interview, be welcoming. Consider factors that may make a witness more comfortable, such as how you dress (e.g., a fancy suit in a mechanic's shop will instantly put witnesses on edge). Shake hands, introduce yourself, ask the witness how he/she would like to be addressed, offer coffee/water, etc. Don't go to the extreme of feigning friendship, but avoid coming across as cold and distant.

Explain the reason and focus of the interview and your role. While some investigators like to engage in neutral conversation first, there is a risk that the person may become more suspicious because he/she obviously was not called to the room to discuss last night's game. By getting directly to the purpose of the meeting, you are attempting to manage the expectations of witnesses/accused/complainant.

> What if one of the interviewers (or the manager who is supporting the interviewer) knows the person being interviewed well?
>
> It still can be appropriate to get directly to the point, but it is often more effective to have some small talk, as long as it is not joking around and it doesn't last too long. For example, ask how work is going or some other normal conversation. If you limit the small talk to one topic, then it won't prolong the suspense.

In providing context for the meeting, it may be helpful to explain how the person is involved ("I was given your name as someone who may be aware of ..."). You also will provide factual information about the process and clearly identify your role as one (a) to gather facts relevant to the incident, and (b) only after you have gathered all of the facts, to make any conclusions about whether a policy violation occurred.

Stress the importance of the witness' cooperation and thank him/her for it. Explain what to expect from the process (you will be asking questions, the other investigator will take notes, the witness will have the opportunity to make a written statement, etc.) and review any "ground rules" for the interview (e.g., an agreement to tell the truth, to seek clarification if the witness does not understand the question, to ask for break when needed).

Introduce the confidentiality and non-retaliation policies, explain that a review of the witness' file indicates that he/she has previously signed an acknowledgment of those policies (if that is true!), but that you want to review it again with him/her. After explaining your expectations with respect to confidentiality (as applicable) and the protections provided against retaliation, elicit the person's verbal understanding of the policies and commitment to them, and then have the person sign a new acknowledgement form and give him/her a copy of the policies.

With the stage set, ask some neutral questions (i.e., not directly associated with the investigation) that you know are true (e.g., employment date, job title) to get a sense of what the person's behavior is when being truthful and to build rapport with the witness. This will be helpful when determining credibility, which will include assessing changes in body language from the baseline behavior you have observed.

Observe behavior when truthful.

△ **CAUTION: No false imprisonment**

Along with the previously discussed positioning in the room, other things may increase the risk of a false imprisonment charge. The obvious ones are those that involve physically blocking or holding someone—this is described as escalation of force in the force continuum taught to law enforcement professionals.[x]

Although it is not to the same levels that law enforcement deals with, any escalation evokes reactions. If the person becomes more compliant, the only concern may be a false imprisonment claim. If the person decides to escalate further, the investigator does not have the resources to counter the escalation and someone may get hurt. On top of that, the ensuing legal action may attract the attention of an attorney who recognizes the conditions of false imprisonment.

Investigators with a law enforcement or security background sometimes prefer to have handcuffs available to them. They may say it is to protect the person from hurting themselves or others; however, the primary intent is clear: physically control the subject. This is another step in the escalation of force and is clearly false imprisonment as well.

With so little potential for good and so much potential for bad, the best approach is a clear no-touch policy. If the person runs away, let him/her. The investigator cannot count on the person to be compliant, due to mental state, potential substance influence, etc.

The other actions that could amount to false imprisonment are verbal. Investigators cannot say things that the person would interpret to mean denial of free will. Two common examples are, "You're not leaving until you tell me the truth," and "If you leave, you're fired." Some investigators will use a written form notifying the witness that he or she is free to leave at any time and has been so advised (see sample *Consent for Investigative Interview & Recording* form in the *Appendix*).

☐ *Interviewer notes*

When you have a second investigator in the interview, discuss in advance what each person will focus on with notes. Whether working with one or two investigators, don't try to capture everything verbatim. One technique that may be helpful is to both have a general outline of the questions to be asked with blank space

Capture quotes of key information.

below it so that the interviewer need only "fill in" the answers. There will be a mixture of shorthand for the general topics and specific quotes for the key details that need to be captured. Quotes are very helpful if the person contradicts himself/herself. Pay attention to any off-hand comments and mark them so you remember to go back and clarify the meaning later (to allow the primary conversation to continue its flow).

Along with writing notes about the discussion, periodically check and note the time. Also note any observed changes in behavior as a parenthetical or side note in line with the discussion. Describe behaviors (body language, areas of hesitation, facial expressions) factually and without interpretation of meaning.

> For example, Michelle specifically noted that Pat, during times in her interview, would be looking at her fingernails instead of Chris. While a conclusion might be that Pat was being untruthful, only facts and observations belong in the notes.

☐ *Recording the interview?*

Having an audio recorder can be particularly helpful when there is only one investigator and to clarify the investigator's notes even if there are two investigators. Audio recordings should not completely replace note-taking, which provides opportunities to recognize patterns and guide follow-up questions. Audio recordings alone also would require significantly more time to review.

Additionally, introducing an audio recorder may have a negative impact on rapport and the person may hold back more. Even worse, a video camera practically shuts the interview down for most people.

As noted in the section discussing risks, many states prohibit recording of another without their consent. For practical and legal purposes, if you choose to record an interview, you should *only* do so with both parties' consent (which you can confirm on the recording). (See sample *Consent for Investigative Interview & Recording* form in the *Appendix.*)

☐ *Pause to control the pace*

A pause is one of the greatest tools in an investigation. Some investigators miss this by trying to conclude an interview quickly (usually to get the person back to work). An average person expects no more than 7 seconds of silence during a conversation and will fill the void. A pause can be a particularly effective tool with the cocky/over-confident witness.

Be comfortable with silence.

Silence—the simplest pause—is easiest to manage, because the parties stay in place. One easy technique the investigator can use is a contemplative look while pausing, which will sometimes prompt additional explanations to help the investigator understand. Another is to takes notes without trying to keep the discussion going, which sometimes will allow the person to keep talking and give info that will help.

👁 Consider Pat at the North Site, who appears nervous and burdened with guilt. Chris' silence allows Pat to provide more information.

One other reason to pause is to consult with the other investigator or call HR if the second person in the interview is a manager—not an investigator. Because time may be of the essence, when you consult, quickly summarize the facts without a long narrative story.

Lastly, don't let silence or the pause have an undesired effect on you, such that you attempt to fill the void with another question or providing unnecessary information.

A riskier pause is to step out, leaving the person in the room. If you leave your second investigator (or the member of management) in the room alone with the person you are interviewing, any conversations can be disputed. There also is a greater risk of being accused of investigator misconduct. One way to mitigate this risk is to ask upon reentering the room if everything is okay and note the response. The risk of leaving someone completely alone is that the person may contact someone else via telephone or text or simply walk out while not engaged. In both cases, upon reentering the room, you can ask if he/she has anything to add or change that came to him/her during the brief break

☐ **Get complete details**

Persistence helps identify incidents of speculation for anything not directly observed. It may also help foresee any challenges the person may have during and after the investigation (stress, etc.). (Refer to *Develop Questions* in the *Planning* phase for some examples.)

△ CAUTION: Don't fill in potholes

When the person being interviewed gets stuck on a word or a thought, the worst thing an interviewer could do is suggest ideas. If the interview reveals a pothole in the path, don't fill it in to make the ride smoother for the person. Instead, ask open-ended follow-up questions and refrain from suggesting answers.

☐ Listen

As a general rule of thumb, you should be listening 80% of the time and talking only 20% of the time. Use the active listening technique whereby you confirm via a summary what the witness just told you. This will help you focus on what the witness is saying and less on what question to ask next.

☐ Timing matters

Generally, it is better to start with a more indirect approach to see what is on the mind of the person being interviewed. As rapport and openness improve, a more direct approach will get the details needed. One aspect of this transition is the discussion of evidence. If the evidence is shown too early, the person may intentionally or unintentionally adapt their story to the evidence and the investigator can miss out on the opportunity to dig deeper into any gaps or contradictions later in the interview.

☐ Consider terms

When conducting interviews, recognize the terms that are okay to use in this book, in your notes, and in the report, can be a

Avoid using trigger words.

distraction in the interview. Any indication of guilt, innocence, credibility, etc. to the person being interviewed can influence his/her story, possibly filtering it to match what that person perceives to be your expectations. Also be cautious of terms like "victim", "harasser", or "perpetrator" which can evoke an emotional response that may affect his/her story as well.

☐ *Ignorance is okay*

Who cares if the person being interviewed is impressed? Many times, ignorance helps the person being interviewed open up more as he/she perceives it as an opportunity to be helpful. Additionally, the person's response to your admitted ignorance allows you to observe the person's behavior and get a better assessment of credibility.

If the investigator tries to seem aware of things, it opens up the risk of presumptive misunderstanding (e.g., "You know what I mean?" "Yeah."). Additionally, when investigators try to build rapport by feigning knowledge, there is an increased risk that the truth about the investigator's lack of knowledge will be discovered through a detail—a person's name, specific date, time, or location—damaging the rapport.

☐ *"Show me"*

Clear communication is challenging, especially when strained by emotions. Words and phrases can have multiple meanings, so it is best to walk through the events in the location of the alleged behavior, if possible. If not, walk through the events in the private interview room or have the person draw a diagram.

As seen in the example with Sam, having an individual walk through the scene on-site also can reveal inconsistencies between explanations.

☐ *Special situations:*

Uncooperative? If an employee refuses to cooperate during the interview (e.g., "I want a lawyer," "I plead the 5th") or if emotions are getting out of control, the investigator should realize that becoming more aggressive will not help. Instead, attempts to reduce the tension may yield cooperation. Further, you can probe into the reason for the lack of cooperation. Also consider altering the style of your questions from open-ended to specific, detailed questions. Sometimes a witness is unwilling to give you information in response to open-ended questions but may answer closed-ended questions. If a witness answers the closed-ended questions with "I don't know", ask follow up questions to probe further (e.g., "was it more than ten? Less than five?"). Ultimately, the witness may realize that you won't accept the non-answers and actually begin to cooperate.

If none of the above tactics help, pause to consider options and consult with HR, convey your appreciation to the person for the time, and address your desire to continue later. Then move on to interview the next person.

Urgent situation? Occasionally, new information learned in an interview may be more urgent than the current interview (e.g., someone else had made a threat of violence). In this case, you need to act quickly. Explain the reason for stopping (just to the level that the person doesn't think it's because of him/her) and that you will continue the interview as soon as can be scheduled.

Break? Most people have an attention span of about 20-40 minutes. This means that there may be the need for a break, particularly if the person didn't get to use the restroom before the interview and the discussion has taken a long time. It is very counter-productive to deny a restroom break and a bad idea to follow that person to the restroom, so the best plan is to have short, effective interviews or—if breaks are needed—keep them short (to prevent collusion during the break).

One way to handle breaks is to agree up front to grant short breaks upon request, but that you may want to finish a particular set of questions before doing so. That way, if he/she requests a break during a critical line of questions, you can refer back to that discussion and let him/her know that a break is forthcoming (in an effort to keep the person engaged on the particular question or series of questions).

Mobile phone? One thing to be aware of is the ubiquitous mobile phone. It often helps to ask the person at the beginning of the interview to turn the phone on silent and refrain from using it during the interview. When unobserved (either in the interview room or during a break), count on that device being used. Really, there is no way to stop a person from doing it, so the only prevention is a good plan for effective interviews.

Fainting? Having Chest Pains? Investigations are stressful, particularly for the accused, but also for the witness or complainant. If the person appears to be losing control/consciousness, stop interviewing and ensure the person's safety (e.g., don't let the person fall). Get some water for the person and assess whether the interview can continue once the person regains composure. If someone says he/she is having chest pains, immediately call 911, regardless of any suspicion about the legitimacy of his/her claim.

☐ **Confirm documents that are evidence**

If there are any documents related to the investigation (e.g., a policy acknowledgement, a note [or email or text] someone received, graffiti [captured by photo]), review them with the witness only after having gotten as much of the person's story as possible without introducing the documents. When showing a document to the witness, ask if it is authentic and, if not, why not. This can be especially critical in cases involving subordinates and supervisors. If the document is inconsistent with the witness' memory, get an explanation.

Ultimately, whether you use documents to confirm a witness' understanding of a policy, learn the sender of a note, or obtain the source of unattributed evidence, documents can sharpen clarity in the investigation.

☐ **Confession**

Some investigators can get people to confess through interrogation. Interrogation is a more complex skill that requires extensive training. Many techniques used to obtain confessions are also positively correlated with false confessions. Recall that the purpose of your investigation is the truth, so refrain from attempting interrogation-type techniques without the appropriate training.

In most investigations, the confessions you get will be given to you; that is, the person decided to give it because of guilty feelings or other factors. Some things you can do can set the environment to improve the chances of a confession (e.g., appeal to the impact on others or the confidence previously earned). However, efforts to compel a person to confess (e.g., threatening police involvement or making/inferring promises about retaining employment) are generally ineffective and usually damage trust, which is particularly harmful if the accused is innocent.

If there is a confession, the goal is to get it in writing and witnessed as soon as possible, without causing the person to reconsider.

△ *CAUTION: Avoid aggressive tactics*

Aggressive tactics damage the organization's trust and objectivity without much benefit. Meaningless threats (e.g., "I'll beat it out of you") and personal assaults (e.g., "You're a liar") can cause emotions to escalate out of control. In fact, a non-confrontational approach—one that is more conversational in nature—typically will yield considerably more information than an aggressive or threatening approach. Although employers do not need to advise employees of their Miranda rights (because the organization's investigators are not law enforcement), this should not be taken as a license to coerce a confession. Statements gained through coercion are usually disregarded by any agency or other body that may examine the case in the future (e.g., a lawsuit or EEOC charge).

☐ *Get it in writing*

Once the discussion is complete, ask the person to write a statement, reflecting what he/she told you. If the person is bilingual, assess whether his/her English comprehension is good enough or if his/her native language would be better. Provide enough paper and ask the person to write on only one side. While the person is writing, either review and update your notes in the room or let the person know you will be right outside the door and will return shortly.

When the person is done, review the statement. The statement will probably not contain all of the elements or details that were discussed, so the next thing to do is a question-and-answer interview on the remaining space on the statement or another sheet of paper. When complete, get a signature on each page.

If the person being interviewed refuses to write a statement or is unable to write due to physical, developmental, or other issues, you can still get a written statement. The investigator should prepare a clear statement (usually typed), read the statement with the person while being witnessed by a third person, ask the person if anything needs to be changed and make edits immediately, then get all three people to sign the document when it is complete.

An alternative technique from Jim Priest:

"I might get an initial written statement from someone but generally, after I interviewed someone, I would write it out in front of them. That way the penmanship is legible and they don't 'self-edit.' They can correct you as you go.

An insurance adjuster told me he purposely made mistakes in writing witness statements so the person would correct it and then he had them initial the correction. This prevented them from later saying 'He just stuck in front of me and told me to sign without reading.'"

If the person requests a copy of his/her own statement, inform him/her that you can provide it at the close of the investigation. While the investigation is ongoing, there is no benefit to having copies floating around.

☐ **Ask the core questions regarding consequences**

Once the statement is written, ask the core questions you developed regarding consequences (e.g., "What do you feel is appropriate punishment for someone guilty of this behavior?" and/or "Does someone who is guilty of this behavior deserve a second chance?").

If the expectations are unrealistic (i.e., too low or high, based on the organization's policies and tolerance), this is a good opportunity to give the person a better perspective and manage his/her expectations.

☐ **Closing the interview**

Ask if there is anything else. This is a great opportunity to leverage the rapport you've developed to find out of other issues that may be of concern. If the person brings something up, it may trigger other investigations. Management will need to be aware, because even the current investigation may require re-prioritization.

Take the opportunity to reinforce the cooperative relationship. You are more likely to get continued cooperation from the witness (e.g., confidentiality, non-retaliation, production of witnesses), if he/she doesn't view the experience as horrible. Stress appreciation for having cooperated, confirm any dates/agreements to provide documents, confirm next steps (if applicable), re-emphasize the non-retaliation agreement and confidentiality agreement (as applicable), invite questions, confirm who to contact with any additional information or concerns, then end on a positive note.

☐ *After the interview*

Immediately following the interview, jot down any final notes about the witness' credibility (more on that in the next section), as well as note any questions to follow up on, new issues that have arisen, or new sources of information. Document the time spent in the interview. Append any documents reviewed to the witness statement. Finally, modify questions to be asked of future witnesses if necessary, and identify any additional documents to be obtained and who will be responsible for doing so (and by when).

Understanding

Stay focused

Gather & evaluate evidence

Conduct interviews

Determine credibility

If material facts are disputed and stories conflict, you will need to make a credibility determination. Unfortunately, assessing credibility is not as simple as it is portrayed in movies. It also is not as simple as watching for a couple specific actions. Most people cannot correctly identify behavior that is associated with lying.[xi]

> Even if a study finds 70% of people look up and left when they lie, what else does it mean? It means that the technique doesn't work 30% of the time and it doesn't specify where those people look when telling the truth.

The EEOC has identified five factors to consider in making credibility assessments, and the authors have added a sixth. No one factor is determinative and all should be considered.

△ *CAUTION: Don't give more credibility than deserved*

It is ingrained in most people—and therefore, most investigators—that people are generally honest and truthful. All too often in an investigation, however, it is clear that not everyone is that way. In addition to outright dishonesty, stories are often clouded by misperceptions of the parties, or only pieces of the truth.

The first problem emerges with the complainant. The first story reported is often automatically given more credibility (i.e., primacy effect); but, just because it is the story you heard first

Beware of primacy effect.

doesn't mean it is any more credible than stories learned later. Watching for primacy bias is particularly important when investigating an incident with widely different stories (i.e., "he said/she said").

The second problem emerges when any of the people involved have a great reputation (i.e., halo effect). This is particularly challenging when the opposing view is presented by someone

Beware of halo effect.

with a less favorable or less established reputation. One common manifestation of this is with a manager versus a line employee—the manager usually has a longer and better-known history, but that must not affect the evaluation of the facts.

Additionally, investigators often presume that witnesses are neutral, objective, and truthful. For example, if a witness corroborates the complainant's story, some investigators actually disregard facts to the contrary. However, witnesses may feel obliged to the complainant or accused, so their credibility needs to be considered as well.

This is demonstrated by Pat, who admits that she was just trying to help Wendy, and therefore backed up Wendy's story of having run to Pat to complain of being accosted by Roger.

□ *Evaluate the inherent plausibility*

When beginning to assess a witness' credibility, ask yourself first if the story is believable on its face. Does it make sense? Consider the statement in relation to what else you have learned about the physical workplace, the undisputed facts, and common sense.

Does the witness give a very superficial account of what happened? Are there obvious missing or vague details? Any significant jumps/gaps in time or details that seem implausible? Are there significant differences in the level of detail, or even excessive detail? Some differences, of course, are expected as people tend to remember some things more than others (generally what is important to that person), but when there are big differences or even excessive details, it may indicate concerns with a witness' veracity.

An example: A complainant reported he was fearful of another employee who was angry and yelling. When the aggressor was interviewed, he was surprised and said they had 'hung out' in the time since the yelling incident (which the aggressor admitted). In the follow-up interview, the complainant said he didn't tell the interviewer about it because "it wasn't fun when we hung out." The complainant admitted he wasn't fearful, he just thought management needed to know about the aggressor's behavior.

The aggressor was counseled for his behavior (versus something more severe if it were taken as initially reported) and the complainant was counseled on the importance of being forthright.

Does the witness use terms and phrases that grab our attention immediately—"harassment," "retaliation," "abuse," to name a few—but fail to present facts to support what essentially are conclusions? Attention-grabbing terms can make an investigation seem more urgent or important when sometimes the term may be a cover that the person is using to manipulate you or your organization.

Consider the situation with Walter at the South site, who complained about being "cyber-bullied" but when pressed for details about why he concluded that, he indicated only that he had received texts where he was being bullied "cyber-ly".

Does the witness side-step questions with a question or by changing the topic? The accused may bring up another issue in an effort to divert the investigator's attention, mitigate the severity of the alleged offense, or justify the accused's behavior as a response to a precipitating event. It may be a legitimate case of mutual wrong-doing, so it can't be ignored; just don't let it throw the investigation off-track.

One common tactic is to make the investigator feel good about himself/herself. Whenever someone compliments the investigator (e.g., "I've always admired you," "you did a great job with [fill in the blank]," "your job is so interesting,") or the witness' superiors (e.g., "the CEO is my role model,") treat it as a screen. Sometimes, it is meaningless chatter to fill in the uncomfortable aspects of the interview situation, but the investigator should take special note of what is discussed before and after the compliment, because the screen may be related to that information.

When a person describes events that are outrageous to the common person, but fails to report the events for a lengthy period of time, evaluate the explanation for the reporting delay.

Also, when thinking about the inherent plausibility of a claim or explanation, consider whether the witness acknowledges any role in what happened (e.g., could have misunderstood what was said, said or did something prior to the situation being investigated). Witnesses who openly accept some level of responsibility, against their own interest, *may* be more believable when they deny other acts.

△ **CAUTION: Misperception of events**

Many experiments have demonstrated that witnesses are imperfect. People do not notice everything (due to attention limitations) or recall every detail, and they often unintentionally rewrite memories. Elizabeth Loftus emphasizes that a witness' confidence, detail and emotional conviction aren't reliable indicators that what they are describing actually happened, because people cannot "reliably distinguish true memories from false memories."[xii]

Sometimes, even independent corroboration is insufficient to correct false memories. Sometimes a person's false memories are so strong, they interpret clear evidence through the lens of the false memory.

> An example: A customer had complained about an employee's conduct during a delivery. The customer told the investigator the sequence of events and walked through critical portions and acted out specific alleged behaviors. The customer invited the investigator to watch video surveillance of the incident, which clearly showed the behavior had not happened; yet, the customer stood next to the investigator, pointing at the screen and saying, "See; right there," as if the customer was seeing the behavior, even though it clearly was not happening.

△ CAUTION: Misinterpretations misguide

Beware of your own tendency to fill in the blanks with explanations that make sense to you and are consistent with your own viewpoint. For example, if a person won't answer questions, some investigators may presume the person has something to hide, when in fact the person may not have actually witnessed anything. If a person says something that the evidence shows to be untrue, some investigators may presume the person is lying, but the person may have a false memory.

Seek understanding.

The list continues, with stories that change, discrepancies in the stories, and delays in reporting concerns. All may provide reasons to be suspicious; however, all may have other possible explanations. Therefore, investigators need to seek understanding instead of presuming an explanation.

☐ Observe demeanor

Use the early parts of the interview to observe the witness and identify the behaviors he/she exhibits when answering the 'easy' questions. Notice the eyes, facial gestures, voice tempo and pitch, hand and leg movement, etc. With this awareness, notice any changes in behavior during the interview and note what was being discussed at the time of the change. Changes

Notice changes in behavior.

do not necessarily mean the person is lying, and may not be significant, but if you observe an individual long enough and compare the changes to the questions being asked, you may find correlation between certain changes and certain topics. Keep in mind that behavior changes may happen *apart* from any falsehoods, because some people are good at controlling themselves when lying, but neglect to control themselves once the need to lie has passed.

The key is observing changes in behavior, not relying on specific "signs" believed to be associated with lying. Current research has called into question whether behaviors such as shifting eyes, fidgety behavior, or rapid blinking are really indicators of untruthfulness, or merely nervousness.

The key to detecting deception is listening, instead of talking. The more the person being interviewed talks, the more opportunity you have to observe changes in his/her behavior in connection with certain topics.

Ultimately, watching a person's body language can be helpful in making a credibility assessment. However, being mindful of the many explanations for behavior, it should not be used to the exclusion of the other credibility factors discussed.

△ **CAUTION:** *Staring is creepy*

Some investigators make special effort to continually observe the person being interviewed, looking for possible signs of deception. The act of constant staring is unsettling in itself and likely would cause a change in behavior that won't necessarily tie to deception.

Instead, short breaks in observation of the person's face allow the investigator to focus on other possible signs, such as breathing, voice pitch, and leg movement. The short breaks also may allow the person to let down any guards that are being used to conceal the truth.

☐ *Motive to falsify*

Discussed previously are the hazards of considering motive too early in the investigation. Ultimately, if you are called upon to assess credibility, you will have to have considered an individual's biases or motive to lie (or even shade the truth, consciously or unconsciously). Consider carefully any personal relationships between the witness and the other parties, any past history/conflicts with either party, any disputes with the organization (including recently imposed disciplinary action), and the timing of the complaints/allegations.

Considering the answers to the core questions on consequences (e.g., "What do you feel is appropriate punishment for someone guilty of this behavior?" and/or "Does someone who is guilty of this behavior deserve a second chance?") also may give some perspective. Look for sympathy, regret, anger, fear, and other emotions and assess whether they fit with the emotions expressed through the other questions in the interview.

For example, if the accused person describes leniency for those who commit those offenses, it *may* be an indication of feeling guilty or scared. If the complainant described heinous acts, fear on the job, and anger at the accused but then advocates a lenient approach, this *may* indicate a false report. But, like all other evidence of motive, do not just assume that; there could be an entirely legitimate explanation, such as fear of retribution, so exercise caution.

☐ *Corroboration*

Corroboration can be an important tool in assessing credibility. The strongest indicators that a statement is accurate is if it (a) leads the investigator to previously-unknown evidence, and (b) provides detail about what happened that is unique *and* consistent with the undisputed facts.

Ask yourself if the witness' testimony is supported by physical or documentary evidence. Is it consistent with the statements of other witnesses? Some investigators actually prepare charts to compare the consistency of a witness' accounts of a particular event against those provided by others. For example, the rows of the chart may identify the specific allegations or topics, and each witness would be assigned a column and in the box corresponding to each witness, you can summarize the witness' account.

△ **CAUTION: *Corroboration does not mean credibility***

When witnesses tell consistent stories, don't automatically assume that the story must be true because consistency; it also can be due to collusion or misinformation. Ask yourself if the story appears rehearsed. If so, you can ask the person to repeat it again and see if it is repeated near verbatim (most people would vary their word choice when telling an unrehearsed story a second time). You also can have the witness work through the story backwards to describe events from the most recent back to the furthest in time. Another tactic is to ask unanticipated questions like, "What was Wendy wearing that day?" or "Can you draw me a picture of where everyone was standing?" Using these methods may help you uncover whether the person is telling you a manufactured story without having to directly confront the witness (which tends to shut a witness down).

□ *Consistency*

Another factor to consider when assessing credibility is the consistency of a witness' own story. A witness' story may change when retold, in minor or even major ways. To probe for consistency, you can ask about events a number of times in the interview and follow-up interview, listening for the details (who, what, when, where, etc.). At appropriate times, confirm what the witness told you with closed, yes/no, questions. Once the witness has committed to a particular detail, you can point out the inconsistency and ask for an explanation and then evaluate the explanation for inherent plausibility.

☐ *Past history*

Like any other factor in assessing credibility, the presence of a past record of similar behavior is not dispositive. However, past behavior of a similar nature is relevant when assessing credibility of a party is accused of engaging in similar conduct.

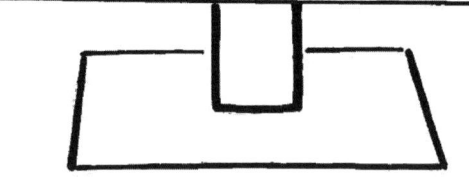

COMPLAINANT provided clear and specific date, time and location of the alleged incident both verbally and in a written statement. WITNESS confirmed the same date and time. WITNESS exhibited signs of deception when answering questions and cried when informed that WITNESS statement was not possible. WITNESS then quit and was escorted out. COMPLAINANT confirmed the previous information, but changed it to another time after being presented with the lack of video evidence. When INVESTIGATOR1 informed COMPLAINANT that ACCUSED was not present that day, COMPLAINANT became

Chapter 4
Michelle Makes Measures Matter

After monitoring Pat's exit, I re-check my notepad, just to make sure I'm not missing anything:

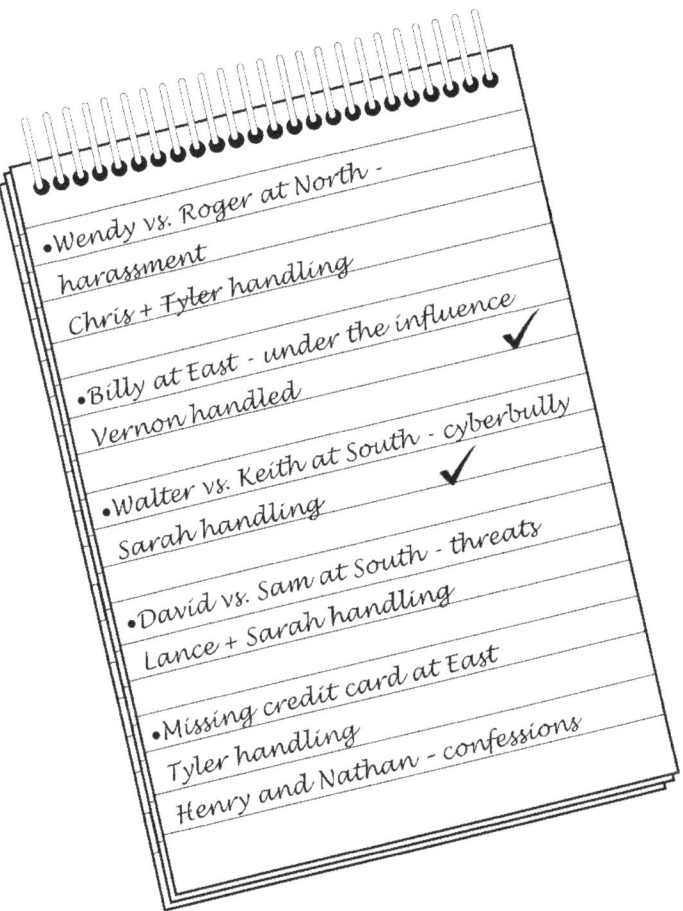

- Wendy vs. Roger at North - harassment
  Chris + Tyler handling
- Billy at East - under the influence ✔
  Vernon handled
- Walter vs. Keith at South - cyberbully ✔
  Sarah handling
- David vs. Sam at South - threats
  Lance + Sarah handling
- Missing credit card at East
  Tyler handling
  Henry and Nathan - confessions

I then check my voicemail. I have a message from Vernon at the East site, asking me to call. I dial his number and walk slowly back to the room to Chris.

Vernon says, "Thank you for calling me back. I just wanted to let you know I was not perfectly comfortable with the interview technique Tyler used yesterday with Henry and Nathan."

I walk with more purpose, knowing I will appreciate the privacy of the room, the implements to write notes, and the opportunity for Chris' participation in any discussion, if necessary. "What happened?"

Vernon says, "Well, most of it was great. Nathan said he knew nothing about what Tyler was asking and Tyler stayed patient for almost an hour. When Tyler suggested to Nathan that he might have just witnessed something and not actually been involved, Nathan perked up a bit and then shook his head a little. Tyler then suggested to Nathan that the discipline is less for those who cooperate. That was the beginning of my unease. After nearly thirty more minutes, Nathan started to get up and Tyler put his hand on Nathan's shoulder and said, 'You probably want to stay if you like your job.' At that point, I was very uncomfortable, because it was the opposite of how you trained us."

I say, "Vernon, I really appreciate this information. Was there anything else?"

"Well, it got better and Tyler did a great job getting Nathan to implicate Henry as the one who took the card and admit that he was aware of what Henry had done. In fact, Henry agreed to share with Nathan some of what they get from using the card. I'm confident the information was true, but am concerned about the investigative methods used."

I ask, "How was the interview with Henry?"

"It was good, but it lasted a long time. The only questionable part was Tyler suggesting that Henry might be able to keep his job if he just came clean. Henry confessed, too."

"Thank you, Vernon. I'll call you later when I see Tyler's report."

"Okay," Vernon says, and we hang up.

Chris immediately asks, "Was that about Tyler's investigation at the East site?"

I sigh and reply, "Yes. We can discuss it later."

Chris asks, "Anything about the interview with Pat we need to discuss before I call Wendy in?"

I reply, "No, you're on track." Chris calls Wendy and asks her to come to the office.

As soon as Wendy enters the room, she says, "Did Pat tell you about what Roger said to her, too?"

Chris replies, "We can't discuss anything about Pat with you; we want to respect her privacy. Please sit down."

Wendy glances at me, then looks back at Chris and says, "Oh, yeah, okay. Well, what do you want, then?"

Chris looks at her notes thoughtfully and says, "Wendy, I appreciated the specific date and time you gave; it is very helpful to have that level of detail when going through evidence. But, when I looked at video, I didn't see anything."

Wendy throws her hands in the air and shrieks, "What!? Are you siding with him?!"

Chris calmly says, "Wendy, I only know your side of the story. All I am trying to do is make sure I completely understand what happened."

A tear starts down Wendy's cheek as she continues shrieking, "It happened! Are you calling me a liar?!"

Chris calmly says, "Wendy, please calm down. I didn't call you anything. I simply said I didn't see anything on video."

Wendy calms a little, sniffs, and says, "Well, maybe you looked at the wrong time. I told you 12:45 to 1:00pm."

Chris looks at the statement and says, "Actually, you said and wrote on your statement that it was between 1:45 and 2:00pm. But if you now think maybe it was a different time, I can look at the video at that time after we are done. While I am confirming details, are you sure it happened on Thursday?"

Wendy nods emphatically and smugly says, "Yes, absolutely."

Chris nods and says, "Okay. Can you tell me what Roger was doing before and after the incident?"

Wendy says, "Well, he was at work, cleaning, you know."

Chris pulls out Roger's time card, looks at it, then looks at Wendy and says, "The reason I ask is because when I checked the video, I didn't see Roger work at all on Thursday."

Wendy stands up and sternly challenges Chris and me with, "So, you are calling me a liar! I'll have you know that you are picking on the wrong person here. I have influence that you aren't even aware of. Do you think you can just mess with me?"

Chris says, "Wendy, calm down, please."

But Wendy didn't hear it over herself saying, "I'll have your jobs."

Chris pulls out Wendy's statement again and says, "Do you stand by the statement you wrote earlier?"

Wendy sits down, crosses her arms, and says, "Yeah, it's the truth. It happened Thursday, just like I said. My time may have been slightly off but it was definitely on Thursday."

Chris says, "Wendy, I checked the timecards. How could you have had an incident with Roger on Thursday, since Roger was not working that day?"

Wendy's mouth opens, but nothing comes out. She closes her mouth tightly, her cheeks flush and a tear rolls down her cheek.

Chris asks, "Wendy, was there an incident on Thursday?"

Wendy's hands tighten around the arms of the chair and her face returns to her usual color. Wendy quickly wipes the tear from her cheek and says, "He has done it before!"

Chris asks, "Wendy, was there an incident on Thursday?"

Wendy defiantly says, "You know there wasn't. Why do you keep asking me?"

Chris says, "Making a false accusation against another employee ..."

Wendy interrupts, "You're just protecting Roger!"

Chris continues, "A false accusation is a very serious violation of company policy. Because you admit to having made one, your employment is terminated."

Wendy shouts, "Fine!" then stands, turns, and walks through the door and to her desk, with Chris following and monitoring from a distance. Wendy grabs her things, throws them in her purse, and stomps toward the exit. As Wendy gets close to the exit, she pushes over a decorative vase, which shatters on the floor, and she keeps on going. Chris says nothing to her but notices two employees in the entry who saw the incident. Chris asks them to write a statement about what they saw and give it to her. Chris quickly cleans up the mess while they are writing.

I call Marie as soon as Wendy walks out. "Marie, I just wanted to let you know that we terminated Wendy's employment because we found that she made a false statement."

Marie replies, "Oh no! Wow, I can't believe it. Well, I am going to a meeting, but I'll call you for details in about an hour. If Wendy tries to contact me, how do you recommend I respond?"

I say, "I do not think you should respond to her at all, unless she threatens to hurt herself or someone else; in that case, call the police."

Marie asks, "Okay." She pauses and asks, "Are you sure she lied?"

I say, "Yes."

Marie asks, "Did she admit to lying?"

I say, "Yes. At first she was adamant about facts that we knew were not correct then she became combative and argumentative when confronted and admitted the incident didn't happen."

Marie sighs, then in a resigned voice, says, "Okay, thanks for the information. We'll talk later."

Chris returns to the office, sits down, relates the incident near the exit and shows me the two written statements.

I ask Chris, "Are you okay?"

Chris replies, "Sure; I just wonder what Marie will say when Wendy contacts her."

"Oh, I already called Marie and briefed her."

Chris relaxes a little and asks, "How did she take it?"

I reply, "She took it pretty well. Fortunately, she trusts us to do the right thing. Now, let's compare notes."

Once we are done looking at the notes, Chris asks, "Okay, any feedback for me?"

I say, "You did well, particularly managing the emotions in both interviews. I liked how you got a little commitment from Pat that turned into more commitment; that was a good 'foot in the door' approach. I also like how you got the critical elements clearly defined with both of them. I think there was more opportunity to use pauses, particularly with Pat; that would have given her more time to fill in the blanks and possibly even confess."

Chris says, "I know. Without a confession of wrongdoing, we may receive a claim in connection with the termination of employment; that's why I was patient with Wendy. Although, we *do* have plenty to support our actions and conclusions." Chris pauses thoughtfully, then says, "The more I think about it, the more upset I get about them. It's just so mean for them to be willing to hurt someone else to distract us from conducting progressive discipline on a tardiness of all things! And to take advantage of someone who is less able to defend himself!"

I say, "We can talk more about it, if you like."

Chris breathes deeply and says, "No, that was what I needed. I just had to get it out. Thanks for listening."

I wrap up my files and say, "Okay, I'll type my statement up and get it to you by tomorrow. When will I see the report?"

Chris gathers her files and says, "I'll have everything else done tonight and then I'll integrate your part once you give it to me, so end of day tomorrow at the latest. Oh, was it okay that I terminated Wendy's employment?"

I smile, "Yes. She admitted the false statement. Without the admission, our typical practice would have led us to suspend her, pending outcome of an investigation. The continued investigation would have considered Wendy's insistence about the date, Pat's statements, and the verification of Roger's absence via timecard, video, and his supervisor, and then sought evidence to disprove our theory. However, in this case with her admission, the facts were clear and you had reason to be confident in your decision; I am glad that you did the right thing for the company. If there ever is any doubt, however, take a moment, step out, and discuss it with me."

Chris says, "I'm glad we were able to determine so soon that the complaint was invalid so we don't have to interview Roger. There is no need to cause additional disruption."

I look at my notepad and make a couple updates:

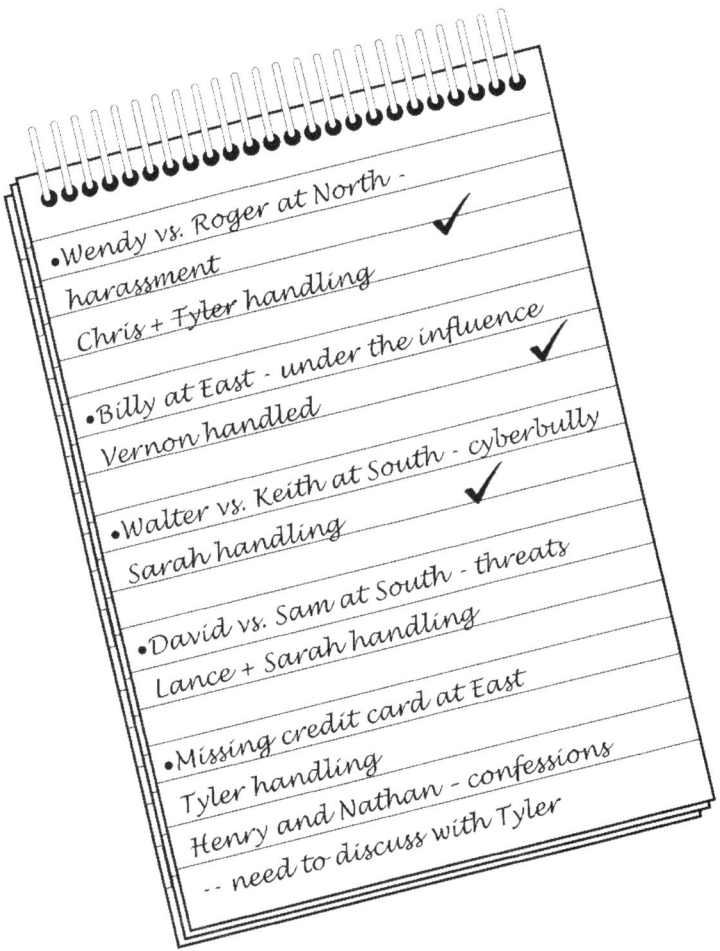

My phone rings; it's Lance. As I answer the phone, Chris gestures that she will go.

Lance says, "Do you have a moment for me to tell you about the meeting Sarah and I had with David, Sam and John?"

I sit down, "Your timing is perfect, please tell me."

"Well, the short version is that David admitted his misunderstanding and apologized for his outburst. Sam expressed concern and support for David. David said he has been having difficulty hearing and will make a doctor's appointment today. I told David that we would get together later to continue the discussion. That's when we will document the discipline and address any possible accommodations. We kept Sam so we could discuss his conduct in the interview yesterday. He indicated that he understood, apologized, and acknowledged the documented discipline for it."

I ask, "So, is everyone back to work?"

Lance says, "Yes and John is happy. Wait a second; John wants to tell you something."

John gets on the phone and says, "Thank you, Michelle. Your team did awesome and they helped improve the employees' confidence in the company."

I reply, "Thanks for the feedback, John. Also, thanks for the teamwork through the process. Have a great day."

We hang up. I dial Tyler's number. "Tyler, it's Michelle. Do you have a minute?"

"Sure. I'm finishing up the report now."

I ask, "Will you be coming to the office with the report?"

Tyler replies, "I can, sure. I'll be there at noon."

"Thanks, Tyler," and we hang up.

I head back to my office and am able to get my part prepared for Chris' investigation and send it to her. A few minutes later, Tyler comes in and sits down.

"Here's the report and investigation file."

I smile and say, "Great! Let me glance over it while you're here." I review the report quickly and see very little specifics regarding the methods used in the interviews. I look for his notes and they are not in the folder. "Where are the notes you and Vernon took during the interviews?"

Tyler leans back in the chair a little and says, "Oh, I forgot mine in the car and I still need to get Vernon's; want me to go get mine?"

I give him a look and say, "The reason for making a folder is so everything related to the investigation is together. Make sure you remember to stay organized. Yes, please go get yours."

While he is out, I read the report a bit more. It seems good, but Vernon's concerns indicate there is more to the story that is not there. Tyler returns and hands me seventeen sheets of paper with good, legible notes, including times, behavior annotations and specific quotes for important details. "Good. Thanks. So, tell me how you got the confessions; that is very impressive."

Tyler proudly says, "It took a long time, but Nathan finally broke and spit it all out."

I ask, "How long did it take?"

Tyler replies, "We were with Nathan for just over two hours."

I ask, "What did you do that caused Nathan to 'break'?"

Tyler leans back in the chair again and says, "I helped him see why he needed to tell me."

I ask, "What specifically did you say?"

Tyler says, "Well, I let him know that his future would be brighter if he told the truth."

I say, "That sounds like an implicit promise of leniency. Did you come right out and promise him something if he confessed?"

Tyler slumps just a little in the chair and says, "Yes, I said that the discipline is less for those who cooperate."

I ask, "Anything else like that?"

Tyler takes a deep breath and says, "When he started to get up, I did say he should stay if he likes his job."

I ask, "Anything else?"

Tyler says, "I said something to Henry about the company being lenient if we get a confession."

I ask, "Anything else like that?"

Tyler says, "No, that was all I said like that."

I ask, "In addition to what you said, was there anything in your behaviors or actions that I should be aware of?"

Tyler pauses, thinking hard about the interview and says with some dismissiveness, "I did put my hand on Nathan's shoulder to connect with him, man to man."

I ask, "What did you say when you touched his shoulder?"

Tyler shows more confidence and says, "That's about when I said he should stay if he likes his job."

I ask, "Do you see any concerns with the comments and the touch?"

Tyler says, "Not really. Look, the confessions are real and no one is hurt. Why should we worry about them complaining to someone? The police won't arrest me for that, after what they did."

I don't address his question; instead, I ask, "Tyler, what is the company policy regarding touching?"

He looks down and mumbles, "It's a no-touch policy."

I ask, "What is the standard discipline for violating that policy?"

Tyler looks a little surprised at the suggestion of discipline, but says, "Up to and including termination of employment."

I ask, "Why do we have that policy?"

Tyler blurts out, "Because you're afraid of the government and lawyers." He pauses, breathes, reins himself in and says, "Sorry; what I meant was that the risks associated with touching far outweigh the potential benefits, and the policy is intended to make sure everyone knows its importance."

I ask, "And what is the primary risk that the no-touch policy addresses?"

He broadens his shoulders a little, as if the machismo might blind me, "It prevents unnecessary escalation of force, since we don't know how the other person might react."

I say, "Right. I am concerned about your safety, primarily. Back to the lawyers; what is the law that I am concerned about when it comes to exposure of the company to risk?"

Tyler says, "False imprisonment."

I look down at the report and say, "I don't seem to see these statements or that physical contact in your notes."

Tyler stands up and with a raised voice says, "Listen, I get it. If you don't want me here, just fire me and get on with it."

I remain calm and say, "Tyler, please sit down so we can talk about this."

Tyler scoffs, "What, are you afraid of me, too? Are you gonna call the police on me?" Tyler sits back down and says, "You don't appreciate that I get results in investigations. That's all that really matters."

I jot a couple notes and let the silence create its own calm. I realize that his violation of policy and the way he is acting not only make him a poor fit for the team, but when coupled with his inability to accept direction in the face of his mistake, also warrants termination. The thought saddens me, but I look at Tyler and say, "Tyler. Those policies are in place to protect the rights of the employees and prevent workplace violence. The fact that you disagree with them is irrelevant. You violated those policies and have further shown no indication that if the situation arose again that you wouldn't do it again. I am suspending your employment, without pay, for 3 days. When you come back on Monday at 9:00am, we'll discuss ..."

Suddenly and wordlessly, Tyler stands up and leaves.

A few minutes later, Sarah enters and says, "Well, Tyler sure is angry. When I pulled in the lot, I saw him getting in his car, so I waved. He pulled up alongside my car and said, 'Tell Michelle I quit.' Then he drove off. He even squealed his tires as he pulled onto the road; could you hear it in here?"

I say, "No. Please write down what happened and put it in his personnel file. Thanks, Sarah." Sarah goes to her office and I complete my notes about the conversation with Tyler.

Around 1:00pm, I receive a call from Marie. "I have four texts, two missed calls, and two voicemails from Wendy, all asking for a second chance and suggesting we can let her work at another location."

I exhale lightly and say, "In many investigations, it's not black and white and there's lots of grey. In this case, it was clear black and white. I can't imagine giving someone a second chance after having lied, particularly to divert attention from a minor disciplinary issue and towards a weaker individual, threatening his reputation and livelihood."

Marie says, "So, you don't recommend a second chance?"

I reply, "No, I don't see any way we can tolerate and enable this conduct."

Marie says, "Okay. I'll let her know when I call her later."

I check my email and see a message from Chris:

from: Chris
to: Michelle
date: Tue, Jul 12, 2016 at 1:03 PM
subject: Statement for report

Michelle,

Please review the below statement to make sure I am on-track with my report. When I think of the extra sensitivity involved in a falsified report in a sexual harassment investigation, I know it is critical to clearly and concisely reflect the basis for the conclusion.

COMPLAINANT provided clear and specific date, time and location of the alleged incident both verbally and in a written statement. WITNESS confirmed the same date and time. WITNESS exhibited signs of deception when answering questions and cried when informed that WITNESS' statement was not possible. WITNESS then quit and was escorted out. COMPLAINANT confirmed the previous information, but changed it to another time after being presented with the lack of video evidence. When INVESTIGATOR1 informed COMPLAINANT that ACCUSED was not present that day, COMPLAINANT became argumentative, then admitted to making a false statement. INVESTIGATOR1 informed COMPLAINANT that COMPLAINANT's employment was terminated due to falsely reporting and COMPLAINANT walked out of the office, collected her belongings, damaged a vase on the way out and left the building.

I reply to her email, "Well done!"

I then review the investigation file for the stolen credit card at the East site. It is a very good file, except for the missing pieces I discussed with Tyler. Once I am done, I call Vernon at the East site. "Hi, Vernon. Do you have some time to discuss the plan for Henry and Nathan?"

"Absolutely, Michelle. I have had a couple people ask about them today, so I'd really like to know what to tell people."

I ask, "What have you told them?"

Vernon says, "I just say that we are addressing a situation that doesn't concern them."

I say, "That's good. So, I want to let you know that Tyler told me about his actions and then he quit. I appreciate your integrity and care for the company and our people; you did the right thing telling me."

Vernon clears his throat and says, "Well, I didn't mean for him to quit; I hoped he could be trained to do it better."

I say, "I understand."

Vernon clears his throat again, "What did he say about me telling you?"

I reply, "You never came up in the discussion. I asked him questions about the details and he answered them. By the way, do you still have the notes from the interviews?"

Vernon says, "Yep. I realized after I talked to you earlier that Tyler hadn't taken them."

"If you can send those over to me today, I'd appreciate it." I then switch topics, and say, "The next thing on my mind is whether Henry and Nathan actually did the offense or if their confessions were false."

Vernon interrupts, "Oh, there's no doubt that the confessions were true. They were each relieved once they confessed—almost as if a weight had been lifted—and wrote their statements. I don't think they would have confessed without Tyler's false promises, but they were true once they were given."

I say, "Okay. Let's examine whether the behavior of the company's agent—which was not ethical—should invalidate the confessions."

Vernon slowly says, "Well, Michelle, it's like you said at our training a couple months ago, the second wrong does not make the first one right ... or did I misunderstand that point?"

I say, "You're right; that's what I said. It still is a good idea to seek to disprove any hypothesis or standard to examine whether the organization is doing the right thing."

Vernon says, "I am a little confused. Are you saying we need to keep them employed?"

I reply, "I'm not saying that. What I am saying is it is wise for leaders to consider the forest, not just the tree in front of them. To do that, we just take a few minutes to do a sort of cross-examination of our values and principles relative to our plans."

Vernon says, "I get it. Before we do something that has a big impact on someone's life and might expose the company to unnecessary risk, examine the plan. Maybe you'd say, before you start the train a-chuggin', take a moment to make sure you're on the right track. I'll tell you this. Henry and Nathan took advantage of someone by committing a crime while working in our building. And then they lied about it repeatedly before they finally confessed. We can't trust them."

I say, "I would tend to agree. However, to ensure that their confessions are not tainted by Tyler's actions, I'd like to send over another investigator to see if they stand by their statements. I'll see if Chris and Lance can meet with them tomorrow. When we get a time set up, I'll have you contact them to bring them back in."

Vernon says, "Got it. Thanks, Michelle."

I say, "Let me know if you need anything, Vernon."

For the remainder of the day, there are several calls, emails and texts as the team learns about Tyler's departure and each person completes the documentation of their investigations.

Wednesday morning, the team comes together for the HR staff meeting. At the staff meeting, we discuss the investigations, what went well and what didn't. I share what happened with Tyler's investigation to a sad and silent room.

We discuss the policies implicated in each of the investigations and whether any need clarifying or if additional training of supervisors or staff is needed on those policies. We also discuss security measures, including an easy re-aiming of hallway cameras, in order to capture patterns, instead of clear pictures of people's faces in smaller areas.

We also use hypotheticals to help us anticipate issues that may arise in future investigations. Chris guides one discussion, asking the group, "Okay, if the customer who had the credit card stolen requests a copy of the video, would we release it?"

In harmony, everyone says, "No." And Lance continues, "But we would explain that we would release it to the police and suggest she contact them."

I ask, "What if Wendy's complaint against Roger had been substantiated?"

Sarah snorts, "He'd be fired, of course."

I prod, "Would that be the end of it?"

Sarah thinks for a moment and says, "No. Firing Roger would have stopped the wrongful conduct, but we'd still have to prevent future wrongdoing and restore any losses Wendy had suffered and monitor for retaliation."

I ask, "And what sorts of actions might prevent future incidents?"

Chris chimes in, "Maybe the new security cameras we are requesting be included in the budget?"

"Yes," I reply, "that could be. We'd also want to consider increased training for both supervisors and staff. Sarah also mentioned restoring the victim to correct any effects of the wrongful behavior. What kind of measures would we consider to accomplish this?"

"An apology?" offers Lance.

I say, "Good, anything else?"

"Well, if she had taken any time off because of the trauma of it, we might offer to restore some or all of the leave taken." Lance says, this time with more confidence.

"We could offer employee assistance program services," says Sarah.

"Right," I say. "Of course, each scenario is going to be fact-specific; we just have to remember that our obligations don't end once the investigation concludes and that the employee assistance program is an invaluable tool."

"We also have to follow up with the parties," says Chris.

"Absolutely," I say. "Chris, what should we tell a complainant at the conclusion of an investigation?"

"Well, we'd report the general conclusions reached. If we took any action, we'd indicate that we took action to correct the problem. Then we'd thank him/her for bringing the matter to our attention and confirm our commitment against retaliation."

"Would we tell them that we disciplined the accused?" asks Sarah.

"No," said Chris. "Only that we took corrective action to prevent future reoccurrence but that we cannot discuss the private personnel matters of another employee. We can urge them to report promptly if it appears the corrective measures were not effective."

As we wind down our discussions of the cases and "what ifs," I take the opportunity to address the broader scope of follow-through. "Remember the training I gave last year, when I showed that clip from the opening of a TV crime drama? The one that opened with one person witnessing an assault-battery-robbery in progress and the witness scared the perpetrator off?"

Lance says, "Yes, and you emphasized the safe distance the witness kept when intervening, reducing the risk to himself. Then the witness called 911 and checked on the victim." I acknowledge, "Right. Do you recall the point we discussed after watching the investigators interview the witness?"

Lance lights up and says, "Oh, yeah! They had gotten the witness' statement and had a good description of the perpetrator. As they were leaving, the witness told the lead investigator, 'I wish I could have provided more' and looked disappointed in himself. The investigator just said, 'you're a hero' and walked off. The witness stood taller, looking proud, but it wasn't realistic."

I say, "Right. The investigator made it look like it is simple for witnesses to deal with the grief, even when it went relatively well. Unfortunately, things may change as the person recalls the incident and continues to second-guess whether he/she did the right thing, at the right time, and thoroughly enough. The investigator thought the job was done, but it wasn't. So, can we apply this lesson to people found to have committed offenses?"

Sarah says, "Yes. Even though we are disgusted by their actions, we still care about them as people."

Lance nods and says, "And this is a stressful time for them."

Chris says, "So, part of our follow-through should be to make sure they, too, are aware of the counseling services with the employee assistance program, because they might not have heard us when we told them the first time."

Sarah says, "And treat them with courtesy if they call us for information or services."

I smile, once again pleased to be a part of such a dynamic and professional team.

Assessing

Decide to investigate

Address safety

Maintain confidentiality

Planning

Be quick, thorough and objective

Select the investigator

Plan the investigation

Prepare questions

Understanding

Stay focused

Gather & evaluate evidence

Conduct interviews

Determine credibility

Completing

Document the investigation

Reach a conclusion

Take action

Follow up

Completing

Document the investigation

Reach a conclusion

Take action

Follow up

After you have conducted all of the interviews—including any follow-up interviews—and reviewed all the documents, update your timeline. At this point you should also be able to clearly identify which facts are disputed and which are not. Updating your investigative file at this stage allows you to objectively evaluate the whole case, determine any gaps, and ensure documentation is complete before preparing a report.

□ *Have someone review your investigation*

After you've documented your investigation, you should determine if the investigation would withstand scrutiny with respect to the scope of issues covered, completeness, and fairness. It is critical to do this *before* attempting to reach a conclusion.

It is helpful at this stage to get an opinion as to scope, completeness, and fairness from another trusted team member not involved in the investigation, or from your employment lawyer.

□ *Report*

If you created an investigative plan and updated your documentation, drafting the report should not be an onerous task. A report can be in the style of a memorandum or can be more extensive. Typically, a report, regardless of style, will include a summary of the initial report, the goals/purposes of the investigation, the identity and roles of the investigators, the types of investigative methods used, a list of documents reviewed, a list of witnesses interviewed, and summaries of those interviews, your factual findings (including resolution of disputed facts), conclusions, and—as applicable—recommendations.

Clarity is an important quality for the final report. Don't write it in the style of a story or a novel, because pronouns are not specific enough. The two most effective approaches are to use the last name every time or to use specific identifiers for each person involved (i.e., complainant, subject, witness1, etc.). Use good grammar and spell-check.

Remember to use factual descriptions and avoid opinions. When you get to the point where you must draw conclusions, clearly label it as a conclusion and identify the facts that led you to that conclusion.

By writing the bulk of the report before reaching a conclusion, you complete the majority of the documentation task. This allows a simple addition for the conclusion, actions to take, and follow-up plan.

☐ *File contents*

The investigation file should include a copy of all evidence and statements. Investigators' notes should be included in the file, but should be reviewed for any commentary that may raise concern if there is a lawsuit in the future.

☐ *File plan*

The investigation file should be secured in a file that is not the personnel file for anyone involved. A separate reference sheet should be completed for each person involved and placed in their personnel files, alerting anyone who reviews the file to the presence of a case.

Completing

Document the investigation

Reach a conclusion

Take action

Follow up

Don't waste energy deliberating or researching every undisputed fact. Also, don't expect to have 100% clarity on the disputed facts. However, you should make every effort to make a decision about what probably happened with respect to every *material* fact, and avoid a "no conclusion" as much as possible.

☐ *Assess credibility and consider intent/motive*

Now is the time to take out your notes with respect to credibility and resolve as many of the disputed facts as possible. As you determine which version of a particular story is more probable than another, document the reasons for your decision—is it because all but one witness indicated that things happened one way, or that the way the contrary witness described is improbable? Is it because the accused was evasive and inconsistent and those supporting his/her version of events were all close personal friends?

If you will be involved with the decision regarding discipline, the issue of motive may play a larger role beyond that of resolving disputed facts. Identify conclusions with respect to motive(s), if requested, and support those conclusions with the underlying facts. Ultimately, identifying and understanding motive after an investigation has concluded can help investigators in future investigations.

☐ *Consider systematic issues*

In addition to making conclusions about disputed versions of events, an investigator also may make conclusions regarding relative culpability and mitigating factors, such as personal issues, poor training, and weaknesses in the corporate/management structure or process.

☐ *Clearly state the decision*

Some investigations are limited to a gathering of the facts and the investigator does not make a recommendation; the decision may be left at the pre-decision point. In those cases, the investigator states the facts as found, and leaves it to the deciding official to make final conclusions and recommendations. In this case, the decision will not be part of the report, but will be included in the investigation file.

When the investigation includes a decision, clarity is important. The usual standard for an investigation is, "more probable than not." You may include the qualifying term, "most likely" when addressing aspects of the findings. Recognize that there are situations where "no conclusion at this time" may be the decision.

☐ *Legal review*

Even if you had your lawyer review your investigation earlier for scope, completeness, and fairness, have your lawyer review the final report with respect to the conclusions you have drawn. Investigative reports may be key documents if there is future litigation, and there is no real substitute to having an attorney's critical eye review the report and your decisions before any action is taken on those decisions.

| **Completing** |
| Document the investigation |
| Reach a conclusion |
| Take action |
| Follow up |

While an investigator may not be in a position to take action, you may be consulted by the manager. This step is the pivot point for resolving the original issue(s) and strengthening the foundation for the organization's future.

□ *Consulting on disciplinary/punishment plan*

It is helpful to consider discussing your disciplinary and/or punishment plan with legal counsel, HR management, and the supervisory chain. Even if the decision is clear due to a policy and practice of no tolerance, the short discussion will result in a better plan and follow-through.

We saw this at the East site with the credit card situation where the discussion with management led to a follow up investigation of Henry and Nathan.

□ *Don't disregard a "small" transgression*

No matter how "small" the transgression, the impact needs to be considered, including the secondary and continuing impacts. Consider the impact on standards, expectations, and workforce morale.

Don't fear or avoid how the decision will set a precedent; rather, consider it and the impact it may have, particularly if there is any disparate treatment (i.e., differences in discipline that correlate to protected categories, such as gender, race, age, etc.).

Also, don't ignore smaller issues when there are larger ones. Just because a person is the victim in a significant issue (e.g., harassment) does not excuse that person's behavior if it was inappropriate in a lesser way (e.g., using profanity toward the accused).

Wendy complained about harassment just before Chris can discipline her regarding lateness. While there was no opportunity to discuss the lateness in this story, there might have been if things had gone differently. Typically, absent a suggestion that the discipline was connected to the harassment (e.g., being proposed by the person doing the harassing, or in response/retaliation for a complaint), you should still proceed with the counseling session.

☐ *Consider mitigating factors*

If the investigation revealed a policy violation, but also identified mitigating factors, you should consider them in fashioning appropriate punishment. For example, an investigation may reveal that the accused violated company policy with respect to disclosure of confidential business information; however, the investigator also may conclude that the violation is attributed, in part, to the lack of training this employee received, an ambiguous policy, and/or poor management or oversight. In that situation, appropriate punishment may be quite different than if the individual knew exactly what was required of him/her but disagreed with whether he/she should have to do it and elected to ignore the relevant directive.

☐ **Opportunity for a second chance?**

When the transgression is something for which punishment other than termination may be sufficient, consider the attitude of the offending party in determining the appropriate consequence. If the person denied the wrongdoing throughout the investigation but the investigation revealed he/she was not being truthful, a second chance typically is not appropriate.

Be prepared for pleas for a second chance, such as "I never did it before," "I'm sorry," "I need this job," "I love it here" and "I'll never do it again." These may be true; the person may have learned a lesson and this could be the great example years from now of the person who turned it around. Or, is it actually just the first time the person got caught? Is the incident an indicator of potential for worse? Is it a rare glimpse into the real character of the person? Particularly in an organization, or for a transgression, with zero tolerance, none of the pleas are likely to matter and consistency will be clear.

Also, be prepared for others to question the decision. One example is terminating an employee for repeated inappropriate comments and having that person's friends decry the continued employment of another employee (whose behavior is usually unrelated to the incident being addressed).

Another interesting thing that may happen during this phase is the presentation of character reference letters, usually collected by the employee who is facing the action. If the letters contain information pertinent to the investigation, then the author should be interviewed. However, the typical letter

contains generalities not related to the incident itself and should hold little or no weight in the decision-making process.

☐ **Document the discipline clearly**

For most investigations, it is best to document even a verbal counseling if that is the chosen measure and include copies of all documentation in the investigation's file, *as well as* the employee's personnel file. If it was discovered that the complainant or witnesses did something wrong, that should be handled with clear documentation so it is not confused with the reporting of the incident.

For the complainant or witnesses who did nothing wrong, do not counsel or discipline the person. It may be perceived as retribution for reporting.

☐ **Treat the accused courteously**

If the investigation was inconclusive or found no evidence of inappropriate conduct, explain that to the accused. Express appreciation for the person's cooperation and understanding of the necessity to look into matters such as these.

If the investigation found that inappropriate conduct had occurred, there is no reason to treat a person disrespectfully, even if you are disgusted by the actions. Nothing is gained—it will not earn more respect and it won't make you feel any better. Actually, if the accused is not treated with courtesy, others may perceive a climate of vindictiveness in the organization that might turn on them someday—even if they do nothing wrong.

Recognize that the person may be experiencing stress and could benefit from the organization's employee assistance program and any counseling services available.

Treating an accused with courtesy does not mean tolerating unacceptable conduct. If someone refuses to leave the premises, call the police without hesitation. Do not allow the situation to escalate and do not believe that you can change the person's mind without things getting worse, possibly even increasing the risk to yourself and others. If the person damages or disrupts on the way out, document the actions and get witness statements for future use; do not bring the person back in to try to get a repayment or have a discussion about the aberrant behavior. Do not expect respect or compliance.

☐ **Closure for the complainant/victims**

One person whose need for closure should not be overlooked is the complainant and/or victim. The conditions that led to the investigation and the investigation itself have been stressful, so it is important to provide the opportunity for closure. If there is more than one person, have the closure discussion with one person at a time.

If the investigation found that inappropriate conduct had occurred, state what was found to have been inappropriate and that the organization has taken appropriate action. Even if it is obvious that the accused's employment was terminated, do not discuss the action or the reasoning behind it.

If there is no conclusion or the allegations were not substantiated, explain to the complainant that there is not enough evidence to make a conclusion at this time, or the evidence did not support the allegations, whichever is

applicable. Encourage the person to notify the investigator or HR immediately if anything should occur or change.

Before concluding the short discussion, restate your appreciation for reporting the concern and giving the organization the opportunity to look into the matter. Also, describe the organization's employee assistance program and any counseling service available. Reaffirm your no-tolerance policy for retaliation and remind the complainant who to contact if he/she suffers acts perceived as retaliation.

Completing

Document the investigation

Reach a conclusion

Take action

Follow up

Even though the investigation may seem complete, it is not. Put the pieces in place that will strengthen the foundation for the organization's future.

☐ *Schedule time*

Go back to talk to people who have actions they need to take or may be unsettled. In particular, find out if the organization's policy and commitment to non-retaliation is working for everyone involved.

☐ *Communicate with organization's population*

While it is unwise to share the details of the investigation (because of the likely negative impact on the climate of trust in the organization), it is good to reinforce the organization's policy without compromising confidentiality. This can help preclude management's feelings of regret if there were a similar incident that followed right after concluding this one and might have been prevented.

☐ *Training for HR and investigators*

Assuming HR leadership has created an open environment for sharing ideas confidentially or you can protect the identities of

the parties by simply referring to the parties by their role (versus their names), it is very effective to discuss the investigation and share the lessons learned with your HR team. The discussion likely will reveal different perspectives about the investigation from which the investigator can learn.

☐ *Control of files*

If the investigation file is ever required to be released, find out exactly what is needed. If the investigation or litigation is not directly about the investigation that has been conducted, there may not be a need for every bit of evidence.

When dealing with claims for unemployment, a summary from the investigator or HR office is usually sufficient. The summary should be redacted so it does not give the names of the complainant and witnesses, in case the information is provided to the person filing. The statements from the complainant and witnesses should not be released, because they usually offer too much specific information to be redacted and they rarely have any bearing on the decision.

☐ *Update and correct policies and deficiencies*

Through the investigation, you may have heard, "I didn't know that was the policy," or you may have noticed a gap in policy that may have helped prevent the incident. While it's fresh in your mind, incorporate the lessons learned into policies.

There may also have been security devices that were missing or not working properly, gaps in surveillance camera coverage, or malfunctioning equipment that may have helped the investigation. This is a great time to correct any deficiencies.

Conclusion
More Michelle

I'm used to having several cases happening at the same time, but I like it better when they are spread out a little more! Of course, even when I only have one or two ongoing, there are always plenty of other things vying for my attention. Because work doesn't stop when an investigation is needed, I feel my biggest responsibility for the company and the HR team is to have the best people on my team and strong processes in place to facilitate success.

It's great to know that my team is so capable, but I admit they are not unique. I am sure you also can hire great people for your team and develop them. Or maybe you are an HR team of one and are developing your own skills! Regardless of the size of your team, their skill level or yours, one thing is essential: a commitment to continuous learning.

A key differentiator between good and great investigators is an awareness of opportunities for improvement. By looking at ways to learn from each experience, we grow and develop good traits, instead of the ego-enhancing protectionist behavior sometimes seen in investigators. As a leader of a team of professionals who do investigations, I know that I have to show a tolerance for errors—as long as there is an openness to learning—for them to be comfortable with the vulnerability necessary for continuous improvement. I believe my team performs so well because of the trust we have in each other—it allows us to share lessons learned and provide constructive criticism, to aid in the continual learning process. I'm fortunate that early in my career as an HR professional in a one-person HR department, I had mentors who created that safe, confidential place for me to develop as well.

The only credit I can take for my team's success is that I make openness a clear expectation every step of the way and demonstrate that example as best I can.

Well, I guess I can also acknowledge the processes I have developed and guided others to develop. The investigation model we use is something I started long ago, and it, too, has gotten better over time. From the practical experience of experts like Chris to the critical thinking and fundamental principles of younger people like Sarah, this model has evolved significantly from the checklist I developed years ago.

To us, the model is a helpful tool; it guides the process. The phases provide the big picture. The steps are a framework that can be a sort of checklist to make sure important things are not forgotten. But that's only the start.

We discuss cases and examples to illustrate the application of the model for training and development. Like the three days I shared with you, real life examples give us the opportunity to consider the model in a more complex setting, particularly because real life is not linear and isolated But that isn't enough to guarantee success, either.

We keep the key principles in mind at all times. In fact, that's how I'll start my presentation next week at the HR conference: The purpose of an investigation is to learn the truth and the primary approach is to try to disprove your hypothesis.

It wasn't a smooth ride getting to this level of success with investigations. Our awareness, analysis, and the solutions developed from our errors make our organization able to fail forward faster. You can do it, too. As good as it feels to do a good job, don't settle for that. Don't get stuck like some do; continually pursue excellence.

Well, now that we're parting, I miss you already ... maybe we'll meet again!

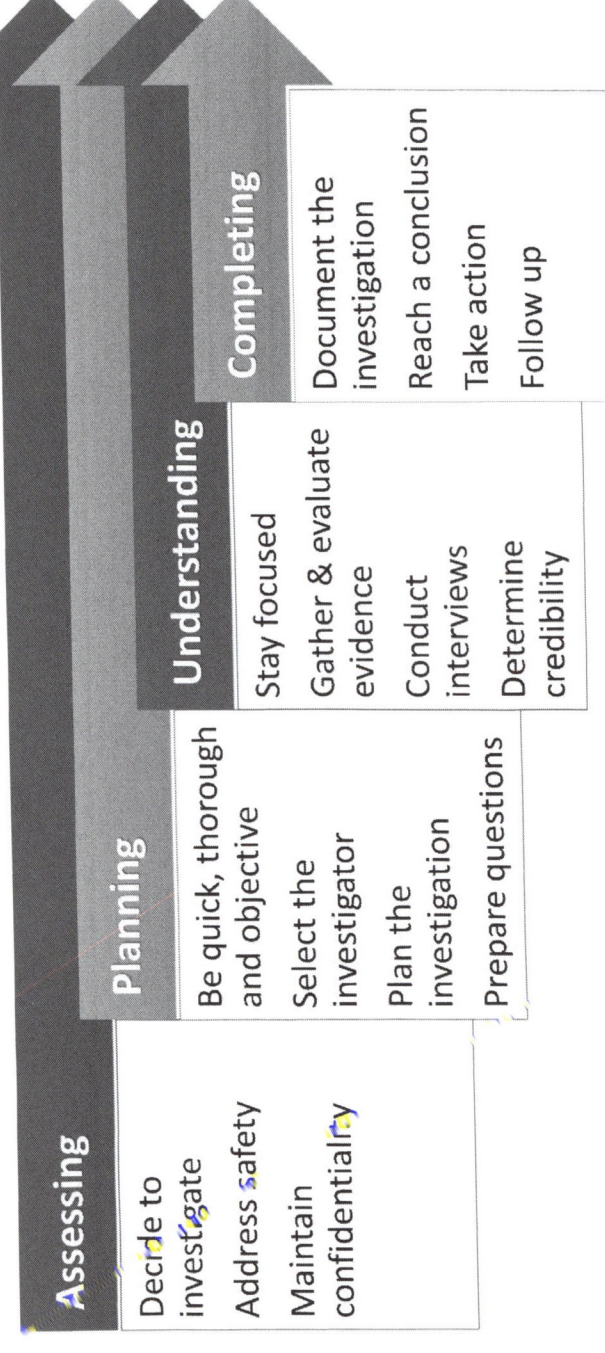

Some Common Threats to Critical Thinking

Confirmation bias: "A tendency to search for or interpret information in a way that confirms one's preconceptions."[xiii]

Fragmentation: Peter Senge's *The Fifth Discipline* emphasizes using a systems perspective, versus "the illusion that the world is created of separate, unrelated forces."[xiv]

Halo effect: "Generalization from the perception of one outstanding personality trait to an overly favorable evaluation of the whole personality."[xv] The rusty halo effect is the same principle for negative generalizations.

Primacy effect: "The first representation established ... is likely to influence the encoding of subsequent repetitions."[xvi]

Selecting an External Investigator

So you have decided to outsource the investigation to an external investigator? Maybe your internal staff doesn't possess the necessary time, training, or skills? Or maybe the matter has serious business or legal implications?

There is a time to bring in an external investigator. To ensure that you are investing your time and resources for an investigation that both meets the objective of uncovering the truth and is defensible, do your due diligence and hire the investigator or investigative firm that has the experience, skills, and capabilities to best investigate the particular matter at hand.

Like an internal investigator, an external investigator must possess the necessary experience and training, must not have any conflicts of interest, and must be able to begin investigating promptly. When considering potential conflicts, be sure to consider your history with any potential investigator and the outcome of prior investigations (e.g., if you hire the same investigator time and time again and the outcome is always in favor of management, which may suggest bias). In addition, you want someone who can communicate well in writing (via the written report), and would present himself/herself well as a witness should the matter end up in litigation. It goes without saying, but whomever you hire should be appropriately licensed, which may mean in some states, such as California, that they are licensed as a private investigator if they are not a licensed attorney.

In deciding who to hire, consider your options. One option is a trained, experienced, Human Resource Consultant. This may be an economical choice appropriate for many of the typical situations encountered by an employer. For more atypical situations—including those in which undercover operations are warranted (e.g., ongoing theft, drug use, or recurring acts of sabotage)—a licensed private investigator can be a good choice. Because one element necessary in an undercover operation is concealing the investigator's true identity and role, a private investigator may permissibly engage in such deceit where other external investigators—particularly attorneys—would be prohibited in doing so. Other situations may call for specialized investigators, such as auditor investigators and computer forensic investigators; although these specialized experts typically work in connection with a lead investigator (internal or external).

When investigating a legal claim that has been asserted or threatened against your organization, or when you want to take advantage of attorney-client privilege (even if you may later choose to waive it and use the investigation as a defense to a claim), an attorney experienced in the law relevant to the claim is a must. If you have outside counsel who regularly represents your organization, get a recommendation from him or her for an independent attorney to conduct the investigation. Not only is your regular employment counsel not considered unbiased, he/she typically will not conduct the investigation because the attorney cannot act as both a witness (i.e., an investigator called to testify about the investigation) and represent you in any resulting litigation.

While the cost of hiring an independent attorney investigator is higher initially, in many cases you will save money in the long run in terms of litigation expense and legal exposure.

Sample Forms

- Investigation Plan
- Investigation Notification Memo
- Interview Intake Form
- Confidentiality and Non-Retaliation Agreement
- Consent for Investigative Interview & Recording
- Investigation Report

Investigation Plan

Regarding:

Opened on:

Issues to be Decided:

Members of the Investigative Team:

Summary of Allegations:

Relevant Policies (attached, including):

Potentially Relevant Documents:

Document	Location

Witnesses:

Name	Possible Areas of Knowledge

Types of Investigative Methods to be Employed:

Risks Present & Mitigating Measures:

Investigation Checklist/ Steps to Be Taken:

Step	Action	Responsible Party	Estimated Completion

Investigation Notification Memo

To: (Employee Name)
From: (Company Representative Name and Title)
Date: (Date)
Subject: Upcoming Workplace Investigation

You may be contacted in the next two weeks by me, (name), or (name of investigator), with respect to a workplace investigation currently underway. This investigation is being conducted as a result of a complaint of a violation of Company policy.

Our company is committed to the prompt and thorough investigation of these types of complaints. Accordingly, we expect our employees to cooperate to the fullest extent possible, which shall include participating in an interview if requested and providing any and all relevant documents to the investigators.

Please understand that this is a sensitive process and the investigation is being undertaken in a way to protect the privacy of all involved to the greatest extent possible. We need your assistance in that matter.

If you have any questions regarding the investigative process, please feel free to contact me. Thank you for your cooperation.

(signature)

Interview Intake Form

Investigation start date:	
Investigation number:	
Interview date:	
Interview location:	
Interview start time:	
Interview end time:	
Interviewer 1 name:	
Interviewer 1 office/department:	
Interviewer 1 phone:	
Interviewer 2 name:	
Interviewer 2 office/department:	
Interviewer 2 phone:	
Interviewee name:	
Interviewee office/department:	
Interviewee work phone:	
Interviewee cell phone:	
Interviewee role in investigation:	Complainant / Victim / Accused / Witness
Interviewee date of hire:	
Interviewee current job title:	
Interviewee currently on clock:	Yes / No

Confidentiality and Non-Retaliation Agreement

I, _____, have been contacted with respect to an investigation conducted at Company into allegations of violation of Company policy. I understand that all information disclosed by me will be disclosed by the Company on an as-needed basis only.

I have been reminded of Company's policy with respect to retaliation. I understand and agree that retaliation is absolutely prohibited and that I will not participate in any retaliatory actions against any other individual participating in the investigation. If I observe any acts of retaliation, I will report those promptly, using the procedures set out for making such complaints. I also understand that if I believe that I have been subject to retaliation for my participation in this investigation, I will report it promptly to the appropriate Company official.

Agreed to by:

Employee signature: _____

Employee name: _____

Employee date: _____

Witness signature: _____

Witness name: _____

Witness date: _____

Consent for Investigative Interview & Recording

(Name) on behalf of (Company) is investigating a claim of workplace misconduct. A thorough investigation is critical to an accurate and speedy resolution of the claims. As part of that investigation, you have been identified as an individual who may have knowledge about that claim.

While witness interviews are critical to the speedy and accurate resolution of the claim(s), your participation in the interview is voluntary. You are free to refuse to answer any questions asked and to stop the interview and/or leave at any time.

By signing below you are indicating that you understand this, any questions you have about the interview process were answered to your satisfaction, and that you have agreed to proceed with the interview.

The investigator is seeking to record this interview via a digital record to use as reference while proceeding with the investigation. You have the right to refuse the audio recording.

Do you consent to audio recording of this interview?

Yes _____   No _____

Employee signature: _____

Employee name: _____

Employee date: _____

Witness signature: _____

Witness name: _____

Witness date: _____

Investigation Report

Case Information
   Investigator:
   Case Number:
   Date Case Recorded:
   Date Case Assigned:

Referral Source
   Reported By:
   E-mail:
   Work Phone:
   Status:
   Position:
   Hire Date:
   Location:
   Employee ID:
   Report Date:
   Incident Date:

Allegation Details
   Case Type:
   Allegation Type:
   Alleged Victim:
   Supervisor:
   Allegation Details:

Subject of Allegation
   Name:
   E-mail:
   Work Phone:
   Status:
   Position:
   Hire Date:
   Location:
   Employee ID:

Investigation Plan

   Purpose:
   Scope:

Case Notes / Investigator Diary
    Action Number: 1
    Action Type:
    Responsible:
    Date Completed:
    Description:

    Action Number: 2
    Action Type:
    Responsible:
    Date Completed:
    Description:

    (continue as necessary)

Summary of Interviews
    Interview #1
    Conducted By:
    Person Interviewed:
    Interview Location:
    Interview Date:
    Summary:

    Interview #2
    Conducted By:
    Person Interviewed:
    Interview Location:
    Interview Date:
    Summary:

    (continue as necessary)

<u>Interview Reports</u>
    Interview #1
    Conducted By:
    Person Interviewed:
    Interview Location:
    Interview Date:

    Credibility Assessment:

    Interview Notes:
        Introduction
            Explained the purpose of the interview
            Explained my role as lead investigator
            Reviewed confidentiality concepts
            Gave overview of protection against retaliation
            Explained interview ground rules:
                Ask for clarification
                Be candid
                "I don't know/remember" are acceptable

        Incident Overview:

        Interview Conclusion
            Thanked witness for honesty and time
            Reviewed confidentiality concepts
            Obtained signature on witness interview report

    (continue as necessary)

<u>Exhibit List</u>

<u>Recommendations</u>

    Final Investigative Findings:

    Final Recommendations:

    Organizational Action Plan:

See The Presentation!

Workplace Internal Investigations:

A Novel Approach

With the foundation of the proven investigation process model that emphasizes critical thinking and risk-management, HR professionals from the full range of experience will gain new perspectives and will leave with paths for immediate success and continued growth.

This dynamic multimedia presentation employs the same approach as this book while introducing *all-new cases* that are not found in the book.   It also includes video footage from employee investigations.

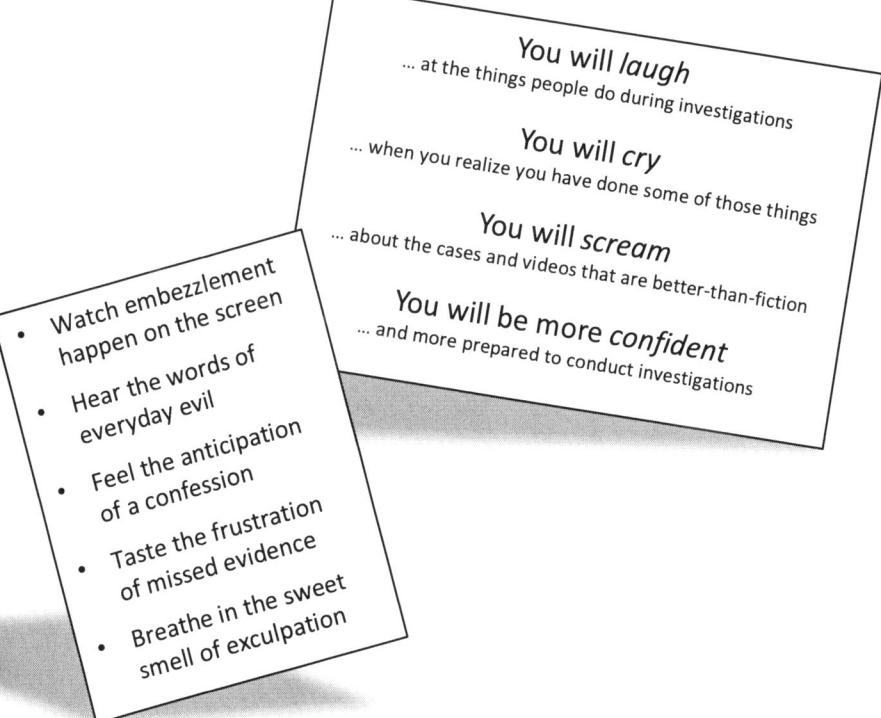

You will laugh
... at the things people do during investigations

You will cry
... when you realize you have done some of those things

You will scream
... about the cases and videos that are better-than-fiction

You will be more confident
... and more prepared to conduct investigations

- Watch embezzlement happen on the screen
- Hear the words of everyday evil
- Feel the anticipation of a confession
- Taste the frustration of missed evidence
- Breathe in the sweet smell of exculpation

Authors' Biographies

B. Max Dubroff

Max's HR experience includes teaching, consulting, as a business partner and as a director. He is also a U.S. Air Force Veteran who specialized in security, law enforcement, and anti-terrorism.

Max served as the Chair of the Central Oklahoma Workforce Investment Board and was appointed as Commissioner to the Oklahoma Employment Security Commission.

Max's education includes a Bachelor of Science in Psychology and a Master of Public Administration in Human Resources. He is certified as a Senior Professional in Human Resources (SPHR) and a Society of Human Resources Senior Certified Professional (SHRM-SCP).

Max lives in The Land of Enchantment with his wife, Kathy. They have a wonderful daughter, Sarah.

 www.linkedin.com/in/maximizer

 @HR_MAXimizer

Christine Cave, Esq.

Christine brings a fresh approach to the legal issues facing businesses today. Her experience spans from years as a business owner, a volunteer on many local and national non-profit boards, service as a judicial law clerk, lecturing and teaching on business and litigation-related topics, and representing businesses and management in lawsuits brought by former and current employees. This experience allows her to understand both the legal and practical issues at play in a particular situation and assist an organization with practical, user-friendly advice on navigating it.

She has served as the Chairperson of the Oklahoma Bar Association Labor & Employment Section, was named as one of Oklahoma's Achievers Under 40 (Class V, 2008), an Oklahoma Super Lawyer: Employment & Labor (2014), and has won numerous leadership awards.

She is certified as a Senior Human Resource Professional and a SHRM - Senior Certified Professional, and has taught courses for a number of years to assist others in achieving such certifications.

Originally from Alaska, she now lives in the heartland of America with her husband, and a menagerie of furry roommates.

 www.linkedin.com/in/christinecave

 @okemployerlaw

Acknowledgements

Special thanks to our friends who provided invaluable observations, insights and recommendations. Your applied critical thinking has made this book more impactful and helpful.

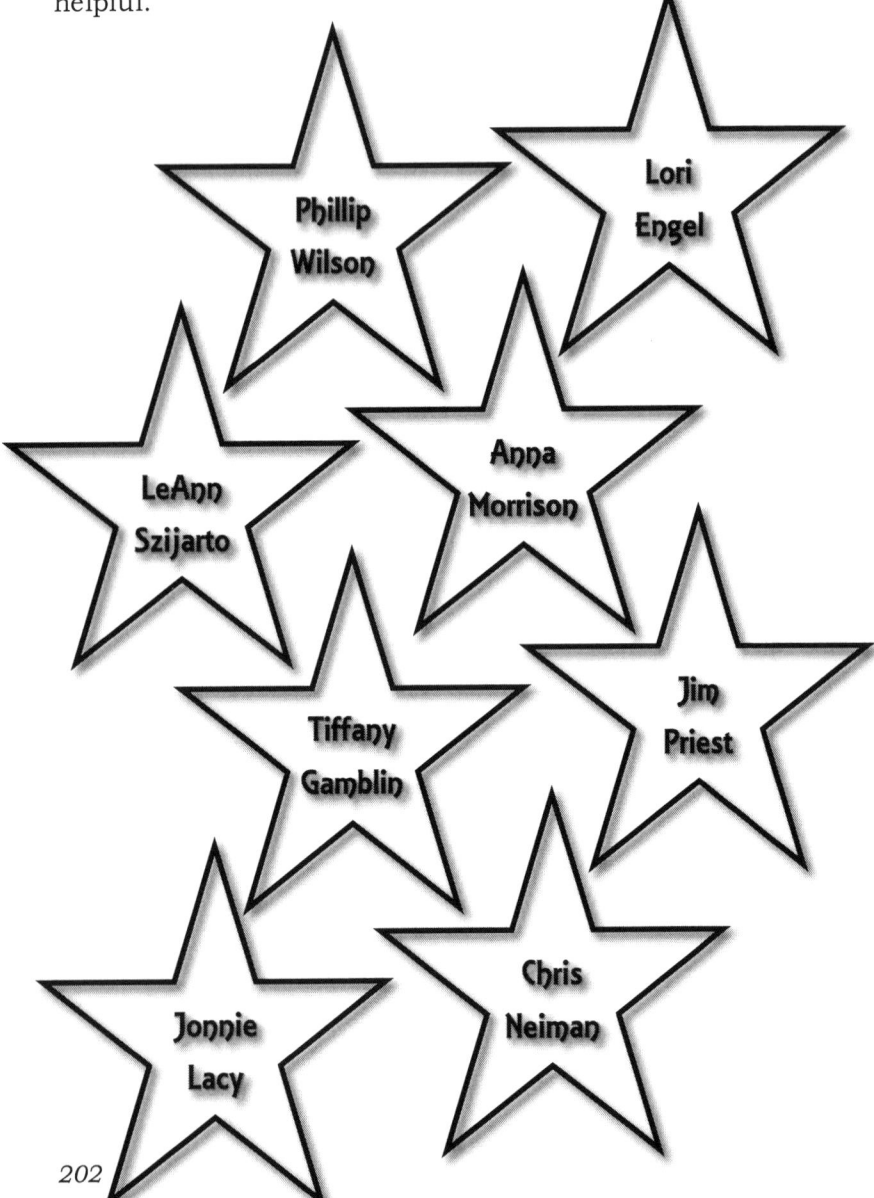

Phillip Wilson

Lori Engel

LeAnn Szijarto

Anna Morrison

Tiffany Gamblin

Jim Priest

Jonnie Lacy

Chris Neiman

Phillip Wilson: Author, Speaker, Leadership and Labor Relations Expert at *Labor Relations Institute* and *Approachable Leadership*

"Up-to-date, practical and entertaining. Highly recommended!"

Jim Priest: Employment attorney and CEO of *Sunbeam Family Services*

LeAnn Szijarto, PHR, SHRM-CP: Human Resources Director at *M-D Building Products*

Anna Morrison: Payroll Specialist at *AHS Staffing*

"A juxtaposition of investigative techniques and relatable illustrations that should help any manager or HR professional."

Jonnie Lacy: World Citizen and Road Warrior.

Tiffany Gamblin, PHR: Human Resources Coordinator at *Paycom*

"This book is a perfect resource to help me conduct a complete and fair investigation."

Chris Neiman: *United States Air Force* Officer

Lori Engel, SPHR: President/CEO at *Ultimate HR - Ultimate Challenge*

"In my 25+ years of conducting workplace investigations, this is the best, comprehensive, awesome systematic approach I have seen."

Dedications

I remember Brian Hayden—a great investigator, selfless servant to our nation and communities, and friend. His intuition and experience were the best I had seen in my career. When he was my lead investigator and I was his chief of security and police, I learned so much from him and was fortunate to be his critical-thinking partner. Sadly, a couple years after his retirement from the US Air Force as a Master Sergeant, while serving as a Deputy Sheriff, Brian Hayden died in line of duty on April 19, 2012. To fulfill this tribute to Brian, I appreciate the support and encouragement of my friends and family; especially my wife, Kathy.

-- Max

As any busy professional knows, balancing work, other interests and commitments, family, and life in general can be tricky. Taking on a task such as this book means that something has to give. In my case, what gave was my family. It only is appropriate, then, to dedicate this to those who sacrificed time and assumed additional responsibilities, which allowed me the opportunity to collaborate on this book. To my husband, Hap, my fur-babies, and my nieces and nephews, I thank you.

-- Christine

End Notes

[i] EEOC. *Enforcement Guidance: Vicarious Employer Liability for Unlawful Harassment by Supervisors.* EEOC Notice 915.002. 6/18/1999. http://www.eeoc.gov/policy/docs/harassment.html

[ii] 29 C.F.R. §654(a).

[iii] *Banner Health System d/b/a Banner Estrella Medical Center*, 362 NLRB No. 137 (June 26, 2015)

[iv] EEOC. *Enforcement Guidance: Vicarious Employer Liability for Unlawful Harassment by Supervisors.* EEOC Notice 915.002. 6/18/1999. http://www.eeoc.gov/policy/docs/harassment.html

[v] Driskell, Tripp and Salas, Eduardo. "Investigative Interviewing: Harnessing the Power of the Team." *Group Dynamics.* Dec2015, Vol. 19 Issue 4, pp. 273-289.

[vi] *NLRB v. Hearst Publications, Inc.*, 332 U.S.111, 124 (1944).

[vii] *Hill v. Children's Village*, 196 F. Supp. 2d 389 (S.D.N.Y. 2002)

[viii] Burgo, Joseph, Ph.D. *The Narcissist You Know: Defending Yourself Against Extreme Narcissists in an All-About-Me Age.* New York: Touchstone/Simon & Schuster. 2015, p. 18.

[ix] Stout, Martha, Ph.D. *The Sociopath Next Door.* New York: Broadway Books. 2005, p. 127.

[x] Lathrop, Sam W. "Reviewing Use of Force." *FBI Law Enforcement Bulletin.* Oct, 2000, Vol. 69 Issue 10, pp. 16-20.

[xi] Hart, Christian L., Hudson, Lucas P., Fillmore, Derek G., & Griffith, James D. "Managerial Beliefs about the Behavioral Cues of Deception." *Individual Differences Research.* Sep 2006. Vol. 4, No. 3. 2006, p. 176.

xii Loftus, Elizabeth. *The Fiction of Memory.* TEDGlobal 2013. June, 2013. https://www.ted.com/talks/elizabeth_loftus_ the_fiction_of_memory/transcript?language=en

xiii Science Daily. http://www.sciencedaily.com/ terms/confirmation_bias.htm

xiv Senge, Peter M. *The Fifth Discipline: The Art and Practice of the Learning Organization.* New York: Doubleday/Currency, 1990, p. 3.

xv Merriam-Webster. http://www.merriam-webster.com/dictionary/halo%20effect

xvi Digirolamo, Gregory J., & Douglas L. Hintzman. "First Impressions are Lasting Impressions: A Primacy Effect in Memory for Repetitions." *Psychonomic Bulletin & Review.* March 1997, Volume 4, Issue 1, pp. 121-124. http://link.springer.com/article/10.3758%2FBF03210784

31048452R00114

Printed in Great Britain
by Amazon